SPUNK

A MANIFESTO MODERNISING FATHERHOOD

DANUSIA MALINA-DERBEN

First published in 2022 by
TRIUMPH PRESS
Kemp House
152–160 City Road
London ECIV 2NX
www.triumphpress.co

Typeset in Garamond by MacGuru Ltd
Printed and bound in Great Britain by CPI Group (UK) Ltd

ISBN 978 1 83820 982 7

To Victor, for helping me understand the power of
different ways to father.
Thank you for saying, "She's like a daughter."

CONTENTS

INTRODUCTION & A NOTE ON SPUNK

It's fair to say a lot has been happening in the world of fatherhood in recent times, as a new world order unfolds in which stereotypical and traditional understandings of roles are reimagined and executed. An evident preoccupation with mothers is easily traced to a necessary overcorrection following decades in which women, especially mothers, were not taken seriously. Even now, I'd argue, mothers are almost exclusively considered in relation to their ability to serve the interests of others. Having partially corrected the historical invisibility of women and mothers through a host of media formats (books, TV, and academic studies, for starters), it's obvious that conversations, research, and policies must include fathers in them as **full partners** rather than have them relegated as pseudo afterthoughts. In other words, **fathers must not be left out**. If you disagree, this book is not for you.

SPUNK is written as part of an emergent challenge

to fathers being at the sideline. It came about because of my experience as a mother and my examination of taken-for-granted assumptions about motherhood itself. Being a mother of ten children spread across decades affords me enormous experience and time to consider the inside of what it means to be a mother from the structural locations I occupy. This culminated in the publication of *NOISE: A Manifesto Modernising Motherhood* (2021)[1], part memoir, part analytic intersectional critique, addressing the many ways societal thinking about motherhood identity and the treatment of mothers needs a radical overhaul.

The journey of crafting *NOISE* is inextricably linked to this book on fatherhood. In my motherhood manifesto, I unpack six culturally significant pillars that scaffold motherhood globally. In taking apart what I call the Mother Stopper Culture, I critically analyse the central question: *How can I be a mother and still be me?*

I began researching motherhood years ago as a tenured business school academic[2], but it was when I started hosting the School for Mothers (SFM) podcast in 2018 that I began hearing the same recurring themes over and over from accomplished guests. These themes stopped them in their tracks or threatened their chances of realising their full potential.

One year on, I decided to host the School for Fathers (SFF) podcast, which turned out to be a significant spur for writing the book you're now reading.

Before I even started recording podcast interviews with fathers, I was met with questions about who the new host would be. Once people were told it would be me, I was asked why I'd talk with men about fatherhood and whether I expected men to speak with me candidly since I'm a woman. The topic brought a mixture of cynical disbelief and serious intensification of fixed beliefs about what's possible between men and women, *especially* about fatherhood. I felt a heavy tinge of mocking underlying these comments as if fatherhood was something to be sneered at. This mini groundswell of questions, consternation and discomfort didn't put me off. If anything, I was galvanised to hear fathers all the more.

I'd realised in listening to women as mothers in the previous year on the SFM show that change, in its broadest sense, couldn't happen without hearing from men as fathers. My agenda in hosting both podcasts was firmly about change for the better for *human beings*, not only for those who happen to be mothers. In *NOISE*[1], I wrote, "*How do we imagine that our children are going to inhabit a different kind of world if we do not give them a context within which to have that world? We say we want it – that different world – but we don't know how to get it. So, we get little chunks of it, but we need to* <u>*do*</u> *something different. I don't have all the answers. I do have the conviction that we – mothers, fathers, parents, all of us – can be the agents of social change our children need.*"

Time and again, questions about motherhood are really questions about fatherhood.

Through hosting SFF, I kept hearing about a hyper normalisation of inhumanity to men as fathers. It seemed that while motherhood routinely features in media conversation (for good and bad), in research communities and policy consideration, fathers occupy a contradictory space. Fathers are talked about as central steadying figures in family life. At the same time, they seem to experience a degradation of purpose in wider society. My interviews unearthed dynamic, shifting, and plural fatherhood identities. Men talked to me about constricting versions of masculinity, fatherhood and work, and the subsequent price for trying to live up to these.

As uplifting and popular as the SFF interviews are, I spent hundreds of hours hearing men's choked voices tell me about their sadness at leaving their children, the effects of witnessing motherhood's toll on women they love, not having anywhere to express their vulnerability and/or trying to learn ways to undo years of emotional paralysis and numbness, succumbing to and beating addictions, and dealing with their own father wounds. Most mentioned the job of growing up, taking responsibility for themselves and their choices while simultaneously raising children they love. Naturally, they also talk of joy, love, accomplishment, lust and pride. But I couldn't ignore the stark and urgent voices of these modern fathers about what fatherhood is for them, what's missing in ways to support fathers, and what's needed as better futures are built.

SPUNK brings together father's voices, data from brand new empirical research on modern fatherhood and advice for building much-needed father-inclusivity. It's an urgent task to set things right with and for fathers, and it's one that must be done. I'm delighted you want to find out more and are joining me in exploring modern fatherhood from fresh perspectives. Sidenote: if you are expecting personal insights about my own father relationships (one bio, one adopted), here's the point where I advise you'll find very little. The reason simply being these men don't represent a diverse or unique enough sample of what fatherhood can, should, or might look like. In conducting the SFF interviews and the research for this book, there were thoughts, ideas and themes that far surpassed anything I could add from my own experiences of fathers and fatherhood – both my own and my children's. These took precedence in the following chapters. Sorry to disappoint ;)

Before I go any further, I want to mention why this book is called SPUNK. Being convent educated, I couldn't have quite anticipated how often I'd be using this word with its many (colourful) meanings. That may be its magic.

A Note on SPUNK

From an etymological perspective, SPUNK (noun) derives from[3]:

"*1530s, 'a spark,' Scottish, from Gaelic spong 'tinder, pith, sponge,' from Latin spongia (see sponge (n.)). The sense of 'courage, pluck, mettle' is first attested 1773. A similar sense evolution took place in cognate Irish sponnc "sponge, tinder, spark; courage, spunk.*"

But it's also commonly known as a: "*Vulgar slang sense of 'seminal fluid' recorded from c. 1888.*"

Linguistically, a tripwire surrounds this word because as much as it has roots in 'courage and determination' and 'gumption', especially in American English (AmE), the British English (BrE) 'seminal fluid/semen' meaning seems to have taken over British minds. Interestingly, many of the other meanings (e.g., 'a spark', 'a match', 'a lively person') seem to be more rooted in northern UK dialects and may not have had much currency in the south when this 'semen' meaning took off[4]. Spunk, of course, is also used now as a verb meaning to ejaculate.

Synonyms for spunk ignore these vulgar meanings and include backbone, constancy, fortitude, and grit, with an antonym of spinelessness. And while we're here, let's take a quick look at three recent examples from online news sources to see current usage of the word:

'And Just Like That…' Is Missing the Funk and the *Spunk*'.

— *Rolling Stone*, 9 Dec. 2021[5]

From Alan Sepinwall, Rolling Stone's Chief TV Critic's headline in an article reviewing the newest sequel to Sex and the City.

'Is this the point at which the Suns are patted on their heads, complimented for their *spunk* and sent along their way into the off-season?'

—*The Arizona Republic*, 22 May 2021[6]

From Kent Somers, neatly melding basketball game analysis and sarcasm.

"The family in "The Tender Bar" reminded me of the feisty Eklund clan in David O. Russell's "The Fighter," minus a lot of the tornado-unleashed-indoors energy that made them seem so alive. Still, there are glimpses of that same kind of spunk here, as when Dad – aka The Voice – comes over the radio and someone hastily shoves the device off a shelf."

— *Variety*, 10 Oct. 2021[7]

Peter Debruge, Chief Film Critic for Variety, on the film adaptation of Pulitzer-winning journalist J.R. Moehringer's memoir.

Why I called this book SPUNK so I could write about contemporary fatherhood is manyfold.

On a simple level, it made me wince-snigger.

Juvenile. Yes.

If only the word weren't so ugly. (*I know, really, I do*).

It sounds like a bad thing, except it's not. I'm certain of it.

It's all too easy to mistake discomfort for disdain. Or disinterest.

So, I started to explore.

First, I thought about *having* spunk: courage, mettle, and constancy. As a child, I'd heard my parents talking about the need for people, aka men, to have this thing called backbone. Yet when we look closely at social constructions of masculinity, we see they're treated as this uniform category in which men appear to "*have been afraid of not measuring up to some vaguely defined notions of what it means to be a man*"[8]. This anxiety revolves explicitly around fear of being seen as "*less than manly, as weak, timid, frightened*"[8], which struck me as an excellent place to look as it appears in direct opposition to spunk.

By defining masculinity in opposition to femininity (which doesn't demand spunk in the same ways), men try to invoke their own version of spunk and gather control to ground a secure sense of masculinity. I'll delve into rigid and essentialist masculine ideals in the next chapter. For now, the overall valourisation of what Scourfield[9] calls the "*essentially competitive character of hegemonic masculinity*" means I'm using SPUNK here to disrupt what's considered SPUNK(Y) for fathers.

Second and obviously, vernacular or slang use of the word is about sperm. The first person to study sperm in detail was Anton van Leeuwenhoek, a Dutchman who developed the early compound microscope. Van Leeuwenhoek first used his new tool to examine other subjects such as lake water, bees, and human lice in the mid-1670s. Colleagues urged him to turn his lens to semen, but he was worried it would be 'indecent' to write about semen and sexual intercourse, so he didn't rush to address the topic publicly. Finally, in 1677, he surrendered and examined his own ejaculate. Van Leeuwenhoek found himself trying to answer the most basic questions: Are sperm parasites or living animals? Does each sperm contain a tiny pre-formed adult human curled up inside? (Yes, really, that was an early thought of how babies are made.)

In 1677 he wrote to the Royal Society of London about his discoveries, saying, "*If your Lordship should consider that these observations may disgust or scandalise the learned, I earnestly beg your Lordship to regard them as private and to publish or destroy them as your Lordship sees fit.*"

The President of the Royal Society (his Lordship) opted to publish van Leeuwenhoek's findings in the journal *Philosophical Transactions* in 1678, and the brand-new field of sperm biology was born. Current day evolutionary sperm biologist, Scott Pitnick, tells us[10], "*I mean, every decent scientist I know has this dogma-busting streak...and so you always have your eyes out for something that doesn't make any sense, that doesn't jive with prevailing theory.*"

Despite substantial advances in infertility research and all the solutions in this area, as I write, sperm research has been unable to develop effective, reliable male birth control. Even though everything from gels to pills has been tried, progress remains elusive. As Daniel Johnston[11], the Chief of the Contraception

Research Branch, shares, "*Sperm are fascinating... there is nothing like them*" – *a* sentiment originally unleashed in a much-quoted Monty Python musical sketch in *The Meaning Of Life* film. This satire about Catholic teachings on reproduction forbidding masturbation and contraception declared, "*Every sperm is sacred, every sperm is great*"[12]. It was said to be the sequence on which Director Terry Jones spent most of the film budget. The song was later co-opted by anti-cloning and anti-abortion activists for demonstrations.

Pitnick, who has spent more than a quarter of a century studying sperm biology, says[11], "*We understand almost nothing about sperm function, what sperm do.*" He goes on to point out many of the answers to these 'unknowns' likely hide within the other half of sperm's puzzle; female bodies. Which brings me full circle to the beginnings of this book through the route of writing about motherhood identity.

New understandings of fatherhood happen when we break open simplistic gendered notions of mothering as providing full-service nurturing and fathering as providing sperm (spunk) and playful fun. Hence, my use of the word isn't one bit to reassert <u>any</u> traditional notion or usage of SPUNK. It's to interrogate critically:

What kind of SPUNK do modern fathers now need?

How do fathers with this SPUNK raise their children?

From a place of subversion and reinvention of the word, I believe a new version of SPUNK is possible for men as fathers. This book will tell you how.

A Short Note on How this Book is Structured

The following chapters are laid out into three sections:

1. **Exploring SPUNK**: A collection of father's voices (narrative blocks) bringing you a breadth of perspectives. These quotes come from hundreds of hours of in-depth interviews within the School for Fathers Podcast.
2. **Debunking SPUNK**: These are thoughts and context around six core pillars of fatherhood that offer a Fatherhood roadmap. I unpack writings from others and share data from the Spunk Survey and quotes from fathers who offer their diverse lived experiences.
3. **Boosting SPUNK**: This is where I hand it back to you. At the end of each chapter, you'll find a short summary and actionable recommendations for those who want to take the conversation further and build fathering differently.

There are several ways SPUNK can be read. You could, for instance, choose to read the sections preceding each chapter in which fathers share their experiences. This will give you a cacophony of different views from the fatherhood trenches. There's solidarity in hearing the stories of others.

You could skip these all together and get stuck straight into the context chapters, which will give you fresh data. Then again, you could explore the action plan immediately or read the book from front to back, sit with it a while, and then come back to the action plan when you're ready. Read it alone in one sitting or spread it out over however long it takes you to find the space to read it – whether that's a week or a year. You could read it with friends or family, or as part of a book club. It could also feature as a dedicated focus in a corporate interest group for fathers and parents.

A Request

How you approach SPUNK from here is entirely up to you. I do have one request. You may have bought this book out of general interest or because you are struggling with a specific issue and need answers. Hopefully, this book will be helpful, but it is not designed as a form of therapy, and I mention this because it might be challenging, emotive, and confusing.

If, by chance, any material in this book raises difficult emotions for you, then please do engage in some form of self-care or seek professional help. This book covers serious issues and is written to open out new discussions. Please think about how you can take care of yourself while reading it.

I'm confident you'll find something here that will become an important gateway to larger conversations, maybe ones you've already started having, or ones you've avoided having. My sincere hope is, after reading this book, you'll want to engage differently in conversations about fathers and fatherhood; conversations that must be had if we want to lift modern fatherhood out of the stunting narratives that have plagued it for too long and into a new, inclusive place. One where all men can redefine being a father with **SPUNK**.

FATHER STUNTER CULTURE & THE SPUNK SURVEY

"There's a distinctive narrative around men, masculinity, what men are, and what men are not at the moment. I think a lot of men are fearful of being a certain way within their relationships and guys are beginning to talk about this more. They're talking about how their sons are growing up in this environment where the popular media are banging on about toxic masculinity all the time. They're growing up in a society where they feel men are being progressively more marginalised. My view on the situation has always been that men are women's best allies and women are men's best allies. It's in all our interests to work together to bring children into the world and bring them up as balanced individuals."

JOE HORTON, Founder of Guild of Dads

"We both get called 'gay dads' all the time, and we're not offended by it, but it has always felt so bizarre. In the same way, you wouldn't imagine someone referring to another parent as a 'straight mum' – it would be considered weird to put anyone else's sexuality and parental status together in the same way. I've done quite a few radio and media interviews, and I'm almost always introduced as 'gay dad of two'. I always have to interject and ask, 'are you a straight dad?' and put that question in their mind. Sexuality, although it is a part of your identity and relationships, it has, perhaps not zero but at the very least, absolutely very little implication on your ability to be a parent and your parenting. Whatever family set-up they grow up in for our children becomes their version of normal. My children don't see me as their 'gay dad' – I'm just dad. While it doesn't hurt my feelings, 'gay dad' is an unnecessary distinction to make."

JAMIE BEAGLEHOLE, Dad Blogger & Influencer

"Part of the reason the bar for fathers is so low is that dads themselves aren't doing much to raise the bar, collectively. Typically, mothers do all the work when it comes to the kids – especially after a divorce or separation. It's just, in my experience, I've ended up being on the other side of that narrative. It's given me a lot of insight and perspective into what mothers, particularly single mothers, have been dealing with forever. It's not easy. I've started to recognise that men need to do better. There are plenty of amazing dads out there, I'm not saying there aren't, but collectively the bar is quite low compared with the standards and expectations we heap on mothers. And I do think there are a lot of men who perhaps don't realise that, who haven't had access to the same sort of perspective as me, so they're not fully conscious of the discrepancies between what's expected from them as fathers compared with mothers. For me, the idea of parenting has always been about having a partnership – it *should* be an equal partnership. But when I'm getting pats on the back for taking my kids out to lunch, and no one says a word about a single mother doing the same thing, you know there's a real disparity in how we view parental roles."

ROB GORSKI, CEO The Autism Dad, LLC

Before we dive headlong into the meaty heart of Father Stunter Culture, I wanted to share a little about the research that underpins a number of narratives and themes within the following chapters. While insightful, this research (like all research) is not without its limitations and it's important to clear this upfront so you're aware and able to acknowledge the data within the context of those limitations.

Having spent two years in conversation with fathers from diverse backgrounds across the globe on the School for Fathers Podcast, I pondered what to do next. I'd not set out to host the podcast en route to writing about fatherhood. At the time I was full-swing into deep analysis of motherhood as I was writing about a concept called the Mother Stopper Culture[1]. It was taking my bandwidth and then some to 'do' motherhood, boardroom consulting, and podcast hosting while deconstructing mothering from the inside, along with writing *NOISE*. Emotionally, not just logistically, it was a challenge.

Retrospective narrative analysis of podcast interviews allowed me to situate individual stories of fathers within their, "*personal experiences (their jobs, their homes), their culture (racial or ethnic), and their historical contexts (time and place).*"[2]

Narrative analysis is popular among writers as it's known to produce greater validity among respondents, mainly because "*expressions of attitudes and meanings emerge naturally*"[3] throughout the interview. I did not originally ask podcast guests the same questions so my retrospective analysis was robust but I felt this couldn't be the sole research method deployed to glean in-depth information on fatherhood. Truth be told, guests spent on average forty-five minutes sharing the interior of their fatherhood experiences with me – their fears, joys, wins, losses. I was told over and over how intimate and unexpected these conversations were and with more than one hundred interviews, I had to choose a subsample from within this larger sample. The guests that feature in this book are diverse voices whether that is obvious at first glance or not. They are fathers who: adopted children, live with invisible disabilities, walked away, have beaten substance addiction, raise biological children as well as step-children, bring up disabled children solo, been incarcerated for decades, work ultra-long hours, are stay at home fathers or have been, raise children with their husband, fought for single father rights, have been shaped by family tragedy, built a substantial business, supported hundreds of fathers, been through mental illness, and more. They are ordinary extraordinary fathers scattered around the world. It's likely that their commitment to being fathers is the common thread although the ways they live this out varies tremendously.

I decided to conduct a supplementary exploratory survey (see Appendix) which was designed to investigate a range of identified topics that form chapters in this book. Podcast interviews helped clarify which topics these needed to be. I hoped a combination of qualitative and quantitative research would glean data allowing a more complete understanding of the experience of fatherhood to develop. As I set out to design the survey it quickly became obvious this couldn't be a five-minute questionnaire. In the end, the SPUNK Survey (I didn't officially call it this when sending it to participants, but this is how you'll see it referred to throughout the book) took respondents on average nineteen minutes to complete, though some took considerably longer because of the mixture of tick box and open text questions. The danger of constructing such a lengthy survey is that the time commitment to do it would be off-putting for some. This was a risk I was willing to take in lieu of rich information.

I disseminated the survey using a snowball

sampling method which means I identified fathers (with children of all ages including 18+) and asked them to recruit other potential survey participants. I didn't ask them to find fathers who share the same characteristics as them (a common strategy), but this can be a limitation within this methodological approach. To gather as many responses as possible, I offered the incentive of three £100 Amazon vouchers chosen randomly that encouraged participants to refer others.

At the close of the SPUNK Survey, 1,333 fathers had completed it. Respondents identified as males (94.5%), between the ages of 35–54 (63.3%), from varied ethnic groups (63% White, 15% Black, 17% Mixed, 5% Asian), with religious beliefs (45% Christian, 40% Agnostic, 8% Jewish, 2% Hindu, 5% Other) and sexual orientations (72% Heterosexual, Bisexual, Asexual or Other, 28%).

Most were well educated (81% holding a college degree or higher), working full-time or self-employed (84.3%) and living a middle-upper class lifestyle in economically developed countries across Europe and North America (92.5% earning a household income Per Annum of over $70,000 USD).

It's worth noting that States-based respondents likely view college and university as the same, so this skews results somewhat. 1.7% earned doctorates, 60%

mentioned university degrees, and 25% obtained a Master's degree.

Most (79.8%) grew up in a two-parent mother/father home, although in the remaining cohort there was vast diversity: from growing up under the care of the local authority, one parent home (mother or father), with grandparent(s), father/father, mother/mother, and with extended family such as aunt. Just over half (64.2%) grew up with responsibilities in the household as a child. It's probable respondents are deeply imprinted at a young age with traditional models of family structure and the role of fathers and mothers.

Growing up in heterosexual relationships takes place within culturally defined social norms that organise sexuality and 'pair-bonding' in Western society in particular historical contexts. This heteronormative context privileges heterosexual relationships and organises gender role expectations in a way that reinforces those expectations. Meanwhile, it marginalises non-heterosexual desire, love, and pair bonding. Additionally, heteronormativity reinforces the ideal (if not practice) of sexual and romantic monogamy, links family authenticity with the presence of children, and implies the need to adhere to patriarchal ideals of the division of domestic labour and gender roles[4].

Respondents answered multiple questions about being a father, whether as a father figure, stepfather or father (see Appendix for the full list of questions asked); 87.2% currently live with a partner and are father figures (93.6%) to one or two children (60%), with a slightly higher concentration of fathers of daughters (74.1%) than sons (68.1%).

The ability to trace whether the children they are living with are biological/step/adoptive/other is difficult within this data set; 78.9% of respondents are fathering more than one child/stepchild under the age of 18 years, with 72.1% living with children more than 50% of the time. The figures do not necessarily add up where 7.4% of respondents state they are a non-resident father. It may be that the term itself doesn't accurately convey the situation fathers feel they live in because the co-parenting nature of fathers lends them to reject the concept. Equally, fathers may have answered no to the question, "*Are you a non-resident father for any of your children?*", as they understood this as a binary divide between either children living with them or not. It's more nuanced than this, hence the need for more attention to this in any further research.

The majority reported having children with one partner (88.3%) with 12.7% also fathering/being a father to stepchildren. Of these modern stepfathers, it's unlikely they're leaning into any familiar family template since only two respondents mentioned growing up with a stepfather. For lack of a better term, it could be argued these fathers are 'winging it'.

In many bodies of research, disabled fathers, as a group, have been ignored. Especially since fathering has been constituted historically in economic and, more precisely, breadwinning terms. Despite increasing interest in fathers' wider involvement in family life, men's relationship to paid work is still centred, which *can* mean disabled fathers might not enter the frame[5]. We don't know the prevalence of disabled fathers. Within this survey, 6.4% identified as having a disability themselves, while 16.8% (across respondents) answered that one or more of their children are disabled.

Limitations of this Research

In order to avoid a sample of respondents that were UK-based White fathers, I screened results frequently and adjusted invitations to participate from communities of diverse fathers. In practice, this meant I leant into my professional networks and connected with influencers and guests from the School for Mothers Podcast, as well as father networks. The self-selecting nature of these fathers means the survey probably contains a group of individuals who are already somewhat engaged with the idea of involved fatherhood and, as such, their views do not represent those of all fathers. As studies have shown that socio-economics, ethnicity and the father's age all impact significantly the extent to which the father wishes to be involved[6], the conclusions of this study cannot be extended to all populations. I won't be generalising about the worldwide father population but rather inferring themes from survey results that may, or may not, be useful to consider in wider ways.

There are some further limitations of the SPUNK Survey. Here's a quick synopsis:

1. Surveying English speaking fathers leaves out those for whom this is not their language.
2. Social desirability bias occurs in both quantitative and qualitative research, where individuals favourably present themselves in ways that support dominant societal norms and standards[7]. Respondents typically do this to guard against social disapproval, negative self-esteem and threatening situations potentially associated with their 'untainted' responses.
3. It's likely some respondents misreported their level of involvement with their children. Societal pressure associated with meeting

nurturant-based parenting expectations could partially explain why reports of fathers' childcare activities could be biased. Fathers who completed the survey may have somewhat overstated their positive parenting qualities and behaviours while de-emphasising their negative child-rearing attributes and deeds.

4. I found it impossible to adequately address the visibility of minority groups in this research and it was a great sadness I had to accept in the end. For instance, the inclusion of trans men's fathering experiences can't be reported here with accuracy. It's possible some respondents are trans men, as 94.5% of respondents identified as male.
5. If I were to design the survey again, I would reconsider the ethnicity categories I used and move away from 'The Big 5' (White, Black, Asian, Mixed and Other) to give more granularity to these. Broad categories like Black or Asian hide hugely different outcomes between different sub-groups and can therefore be misleading. It's important to note these limitations and, in particular, that data for an aggregated group (the Black group, for example) can mask differences in outcomes for

detailed ethnic groups (the Black Caribbean and Black African groups, for example).

6. I followed typical classification of fathers who do not live full-time with their children as either 'resident' or 'non-resident' but found this limited understanding and investigation. Basic classification masks a wide range of care-and-contact patterns. For example, no-contact, daytime care, minority overnight care (one or two nights a week), equal overnight care, majority overnight care, living part-time in the child's household, and temporary longer-term non-residence with the child. Better differentiation between residence patterns of fathers would have definitely helped.

When I was an academic, I (co)designed research projects and taught postgraduates research methodology as part of my work. Publishing in the Academy of Management Journal (AMJ) on cross-cultural research methodological issues (breaking ground on gender and race) was arguably a career highlight of mine[8]. So, when I began to receive a clutch of emails like the below, I wondered what it meant:

Danusia, I took your fatherhood survey and the

questions about the number of children and being a father/father figure is confusing. Maybe rethink it, is the design right?
David

Dear Danusia, I'm not sure how to answer how many kids I'm a father to? It's complicated. You could leave it at the do you have children Yes/No, then it would be easy to answer. Let me know when you do this.
Cheers. Brad

Far from getting concerned about the rigour of survey design (several weeks leading a specialist academic team crafting it left me confident) I was delighted to be uncovering layers of nuance about being a father a more simplistic approach couldn't get to. I'll deal with what these queries were really getting at in later chapters, but essentially some respondents were finding it hard to navigate who they consider themselves father to/for. It was an unexpected bonus to receive not only queries about the number and status of children but also #surveydesign101 mansplaining advice. Rebecca Solnit coined the term originally and outlines it beautifully in her follow up essay, *Men Still Explain Things to Me*[9]. Suffice to say, these injections of information told me more about respondents and the subject itself than contributing towards any survey design self-doubts I might be harbouring. Point is, these emails happened. I wonder if men would have felt quite so emboldened to proffer such feedback had I been the owner of a penis.

The answer is they wouldn't.

Father Stunter Culture & the Masculinity Crisis

Much has been written about a general 'crisis of masculinity', but most especially about the toxic forces of collective masculinity. Coined in the late twentieth century, the concept of 'toxic masculinity' spread to therapeutic and social policy settings in the early twenty-first century. But since 2013, feminists have begun attributing misogyny, homophobia, and men's violence to the concept, though it is often left under-defined[10].

In an analysis of the emergence of the phrase 'toxic masculinity', Carol Harrington, who has taught on gender-based violence since 2000, found that between 1990 and 2015, texts referring to toxic masculinity never numbered above twenty a year. From 2017, thousands of references to this concept began to appear, mainly non-academic texts. This corresponded with Merriam Webster's top *Word of the Year*[11], feminism – a whopping 70% search increase from 2016 – alongside an upsurge in women's accounts of sexual assault and harassment, and (as a result) the birth of the #MeToo movement. Meanwhile, 'toxic' was voted *Word of the Year* in 2018 by Oxford University Press.

In an article[12] about the need for more feminist dads, Jordan Shapiro shares how a toxic masculinity diagnosis was formalised when the American Psychological Association issued its first *Guidelines for Psychological Practice with Boys and Men*. That document frames the concept as men being "*so afraid of appearing weak or "feminine" that they bury their feelings; they over-conceal. This can lead to mental health issues, cardiovascular problems, substance abuse, violence, incarceration, early mortality, and more.*"

But there are several criticisms of the concept, not least that it's commonly used without a systematic and stable definition. Indeed, in an article on family therapy from 2002, Dollahite, Marks, and Olsonm[13] argued the phrase was becoming, "*part and parcel of scholarly and popular clinical literature*" that represented a "*deficit perspective*" toward men. An emerging tendency to see maleness as a problem was set.

Originally, and arguably, wrongly associated with 'marginalised men' (low income, ill-educated, out of work, minorities, absent fathers), toxic masculinity has spread to include men as a homogenised group. I'm not saying toxic masculinity has spread to all men. I AM saying that few men (if any) are left untouched by this cultural tipping point within a context of societal perceptions about maleness.

What's common across the discussion of masculinity is downright disapproval. Or as Norah Vincent, who spent a year disguised as a man learning the unspoken codes of male experience, says[14], "*Manhood is a leaden mythology riding on the shoulders of every man…we feel no political sympathy for "man" because he has been… the collective nightmare sitting on our chest.*"

If I look at the core idea surrounding toxic masculinity and fathers, it goes like this: emotionally distant authoritarian fathers in Western culture hand down negative versions of masculinity that produce boys who go on to do the same. Male children are offered – more force-fed – models, rules and regulations that lock them into a false, limiting framework of manhood and fix in place an extraordinarily narrow band of operational masculinity. These become "*unconscious, dogmatic operating principles*"[15] and continue generationally. If we synthesise work by researchers Heilman[16] and Morin[17] to carve out three components of toxic masculinity, the following become clear (but are by no means exhaustive):

1. **Toughness:** the notion that men should be physically strong, emotionally cool, if not callous, and behaviourally aggressive. They should display self-sufficiency, act tough and use aggression to resolve conflicts.
2. **Anti-Femininity:** the idea that men should reject anything that's considered to be feminine, such as showing emotion or accepting help. This also includes a specific 'masculine' physique involving muscle and body bulk.
3. **Power:** the assumption that men must work toward obtaining power and status (social and financial) to gain the respect of others. This includes sticking to rigid gender roles, being unambiguously heterosexual, and always ready for sex.

No wonder it's said, "*masculinity is a hard, small cage, and we put boys inside this cage.*"[18] These same boys become grown men. At which point that rigid small cage becomes what many call the 'Man Box'[16]; a shorthand phrase for those narrow internally contradictory mainstream ideas on what it means to "*man up*" or be a "*real man*". It's called a box because restrictive and equally strict definitions of what it takes to "*be a man*" prevent men from expressing their individuality and positive instincts. Instead, they're crammed into a reductive box and penalised socially for any transgressions against these mainstream notions.

Gender roles (for men and women) are seen as confinements that trap them in socially, politically or biologically determined power structures. While the cage/box for men is generally described as larger and better furnished, it's a cage, nonetheless. This brings us back to the notion of a masculinity crisis, or rather, as Robert Webb jokes in his book, *How Not to Be a Boy*[19], not masculinity ***in*** crisis but rather that masculinity ***is*** a crisis. Although he takes this joke back fast, it can hardly be a surprise that, as Michael Kimmel writes[20], "*Men are in power, everyone agrees, but when you say therefore men must feel powerful, they look at you cross-eyed. They say, "What are you talking about? I have no power. My wife bosses me around. My kids boss me around. My boss bosses me around...All of the power in the world has not trickled down to individual men feeling powerful.*"

Which points to the differences between social and individual power because while patriarchy is not simply men's power over women, it's also some men's power over other men. Patriarchy's a dual system of power. Unless we grasp this, we won't understand why so many men feel like they're complete losers in the gender game and not at all privileged. These men, from this misunderstood space, resist efforts toward gender equality. Michael Kimmel is hopeful "*we can make them allies,*" but only if we scrap the notion of a healthy/unhealthy (toxic) dichotomy of masculinity: "*They're too afraid to let go of things because **you** think they're unhealthy.*"[20]

One suggested way forward or 'cure' for toxic maleness has been for young boys to receive and learn from 'mature' versions of masculinity via father figures and mentors, albeit where these spring from isn't exactly clear. An Irish family policy article suggested engaging men in fatherhood itself so that men's "*wildness is tamed to the extent that they can adjust to the discipline of domestic routines and remain with their children and partners and in their families (as opposed to prison, for instance).*"[21] Essentialist notions about men's inherent need to be tamed are strong in this particular suggestion!

Liberating men from toxic masculinity is not viewed as the solution since some oppose any amendment of masculinity and recognise that such toxic masculinity is socially constructed. Glen Poole argues[22] it's not the culture of traditional masculinity that's at fault. It's the culture which he claims seeks to censor it, "*it's not a "macho culture" that prevents men from "speaking out"; it's a culture that isn't yet "man enough" to listen and respond to men's needs."* For Poole, it's the denigration of 'real' men that's at the heart of a crisis of masculinity.

For sure, narratives of men, masculinity and crisis are tricky and not one bit straightforward. You'll note I'm sidestepping pinning my stake in the ground, for good reason. As a cisgender hetero-white woman with history with my own father(s), children's father(s), and a wealth of lived experience around men as fathers, I oscillate back, forth, to, fro. As I write this, I'm aware I lay myself open because even as I craft this book, I'm doing so through a lens of what feels like pseudo masculinity. To be decisive is often 'masculine' as is leading and leadership. Critique of this is possible because decision making and leadership are <u>not</u> the natural domains of men. *Bear with me.*

To share vulnerably with you that I'm cognizant I'm failing to take a firm position on toxic masculinity feels dangerous. To build authority as a writer, we have to take sides. Note this as you consider my lack here; both vulnerability and failing are not allowable in prescriptive scripts about being a 'real' man. I'm <u>not male,</u> but in writing a book on fatherhood as a woman, and as the host of a podcast interviewing men as fathers, I'm <u>not unmeshed</u> from the strictures that bind men to versions of success. This patriarchal world undervalues attributes seen as feminine, which I'm intentionally displaying and sharing.

Let me repeat this and be clear: to display a lack of knowledge translates into a failure of authority, which in turn reduces power. To admit to this is tantamount to a suicide of sorts. Instead, a reverence for blagging bullshit and a pretence mask is a preferred 'masculine' tactic that at least garners some level of respect. I'm rejecting that. But of course, not wholly. To unpack this process while writing a book on men as fathers gives me a tiny inkling of how it might feel to navigate the rewards and punishments of contradictory ideals; for people navigating the confines of masculinity and for me, navigating being a woman analysing masculinity and fatherhood.

In writing about masculinity, I find it easy to access deep compassion about the extent to which men are locked into versions of masculinity that constrict and stifle them. I also recognise (many of them) are simultaneously afforded privilege and opportunity because of their maleness. Thinly veiled disdain is also present here for me too. As a mother of ten, six of whom are sons, I've raised four to adult age and witnessed the horrifying impacts of my boys trying to shoehorn themselves into 'being real men'. I've seen each attacked psychologically and physically by other males, and, in varying ways, how each navigate(d) masculine rules that make/made them experience and perpetrate violence, especially to themselves. It is not one or the other; it's both. As feminist and civil rights scholar, bell hooks writes[23]: "*Patriarchy demands of all males that they engage in acts of psychic self-mutilation, that they kill off the emotional parts of themselves. If a man is not successful in emotionally crippling himself, he can count on patriarchal men to enact rituals of power that will assault his self-esteem.*"

I've also witnessed profound differences between raising girls *vis a vis* boys. Boys have not always been considered as needing support as a better understanding of the contradictory mechanisms deployed within patriarchy have unfolded.

Gender and masculinity are always subject to internal contradiction and flux, and most importantly, the category of 'men' is not uniform. There are differences <u>between</u> men and there are multiple symbolic constructions of masculinity. The 'masculinity' said to be in crisis is often implicitly assumed to be middle-class, White, and heterosexual, constructing men, "*as an homogenous group lacking class, ethnic, sexual or racial differentiation*"[24]. A fundamental lack of recognition of the hierarchical positioning of different groups of men within the gender order is not just an oversight in crisis-of-masculinity narratives but a result of the framing of the crisis of masculinity itself. The notion of crisis constructs masculinity as singular rather than multiple, and in doing so, implies not only that masculinity is a fixed property of men but also that men are a uniform group. It's evident men can never be this because race and ethnicity play a crucial role in how men view their and others masculinity.

All this has enormous significance for men as fathers. First though, let's look at what we mean by the terms father, fatherhood, and fathering.

The word father (noun) is defined as "*a male parent*" while the verb of the same word means, "*to become the father of a child by making a woman pregnant*"[25]; gender-specific and traditional, right?! Equally, a mother (noun) by definition is "*a woman in relation to her child or children*". The *verb* of mother means "*to bring up (a child) with care and affection*"[26]; an ungendered meaning and one that doesn't need to be performed by a child's mother. Anyone can offer care and affection.

We've inscribed the notion of mother with certain traits. We denote it with these ways of being, but I question whether there's any reason why a man can't be a mother? Except for that cisgender heteronormative couples and cultures define mothering as women's work of the type 'real men' ought to distance from. More often than not, women bear the lion's share of childcare and parenting responsibilities – even, if not especially – when a man is present. Childcare is gendered work, seen as the province of those who are female. So, while it is important to recognise that a biological or social male *can* assume the role of 'mother', it's equally important to recognise the profoundly gendered division of labour in the domestic sphere, which we'll explore in chapter three.

Nevertheless, isn't it fascinating that 'father' refers to the connection between a particular child and a particular man (whether biological or social)? Whereas 'mother' refers to "*her child or children*", implying an intimate connection that's missing within the father definition.

Earlier this year, The Australian National University (ANU) Gender Institute suggested ditching words such as mother and father to be more gender inclusive. In their Gender-Inclusive Handbook[27], *Every Voice Project,* the ANU recommend changing the term 'mother' to "*gestational*" or "*birthing parent*" and using "*non-gestational*" or "*non-birthing parent*" instead of 'father'. The guide suggests that non-gendered language is particularly important in clinical discussions of childbirth and parenthood and helps model inclusive behaviour for all. This guide is not yet an official ANU policy, process or official prescription but is instead seen as recommendations to staff and students. This Australian guide followed UK's The Brighton and Sussex University Hospital (BSUH) NHS Trust's introduction of measures to be more inclusive towards non-cisgender, trans and non-binary families. As part of this, 'breastfeeding' was changed to "*chestfeeding*". Significantly, the term 'father' was also changed to "*second biological parent*" or "*co-parent*", while the term 'woman' was adjusted to include "*woman or person*".

Is it me, or does the change from 'father' to 'second biological parent' include a backhanded swipe of sorts? Baffling. Though I'm in principle not against de-genderising the term, I AM calling into question why BSUH would place a 'numbered position' on a parent. What could be the rationale for fathers being **secondary**? Are we left to assume that 'mother' is now 'first biological parent' or do they get to be called something else? Readers, at the time of writing, I couldn't discover the answer to this language conundrum.

Fathering seems to have two fundamental meanings. The first means "*bring into being, bring into the world, give life to*", which we could be forgiven for seeing as donating sperm to create new life. And the second meaning is "*to be the father of...*" as in "*treat with the protective care associated with a father.*"[25] In essence, this refers to behaviour, the actual practices of 'doing' parenting. Mothering is framed too, as a practice and described as work 'mothering people' engage in when they set out to fulfil the demands of mother work (nurturing, protection, training and cultural bearing[28]). If we are to understand fathering, it feels vital to extrapolate the core activities of what fathering someone actually is, from what modern fatherhood has been packaged into. I intend to unfurl fixed ideas of father and the activity of fathering as we move further into this book.

And finally, fatherhood is defined as a cultural and social institution that includes the rights, duties, responsibilities, and statuses associated with being a father. This is both general ideologies as well as public meanings associated with being a father[25].

If I've learned anything in researching fatherhood, it's that the time is long overdue for a revolutionary departure from hegemonic masculinity so a refashioned fatherhood roadmap can be constructed. This will take **SPUNK**. The kind that uses learning from dominant notions of manliness while revisioning progressive approaches to the way forward. It's not as if this isn't already happening as <u>individual</u> men try to find ways to straddle the demands of masculinity and fatherhood. Sometimes these individuals join together to voice the countercurrent job of confronting 'manhood as usual'. SPUNK is needed in a culture that doesn't want fathers to be whole, complete human beings. I've come to call this culture the **Father Stunter Culture**.

Father Stunters are those people who assume men babysit their own children and congratulate them for their daddy daycare sessions. They're the women who 'helpfully' assume fathers cannot cope and swoop in to do the job of caring for their child 'properly'. Father Stunters count fathers as one of the kids because "*you're a man and what would you know?!*" They're workplace managers jumping to conclusions about a father's commitment to their family and mental health as less than to their career. They're educational and medical processes that place fathers as footnotes in children's lives. They're experts on paternity (and maternity), baby kits, baby sleeping, child psycho-social-emotional development, birthing, and paternity advice – and that's just the beginning. Father Stunters categorise fathers as one of only a narrow index of men. From feckless fathers, workaholic fathers, playful pop, deadbeat dads, cool dads, missing in action fathers – and so it goes on.

Many say men don't experience Father Stunters but take a look; father stunting is everywhere. In the media, within headlines, in drama scripts, the way advertisements are structured, social policies that make it impossible for men to take paternity leave, laws designed to show that breadwinning is a father's most significant contribution, post-separation child access orders that assume mothers are primary parents – the list is endless. Father Stunters force the bar low for men as fathers.

Father Stunters aren't just 'people' and they keep on coming; paternal leave-provider dilemmas; educational hours operating on assumptions of one parent (assumed to be the mother) available for caregiving; lack of affordable childcare or availability of childcare, no-one to confide in, financial pressure and economic instability; bouts of depression triggered by family and personal losses; substance abuse challenges and physical health ailments – amongst so many other potential stunters. But let's not blanket this; Father Stunters aren't the same for everyone. The intersections of race, gender, sexuality and class-based oppression – both historical and contemporary – contribute to distinct fatherhood experiences. For example, few studies on Black fatherhood have examined how Black fathers understand their roles and responsibilities as parents, especially those that may challenge traditional, heterosexual norms of fatherhood[29].

In the following chapters, I'll share fresh empirical

data from fathers' experience of the Father Stunter Culture to lay out the roadmap. Barack Obama spoke gold when he said[30]: "*Sadly in our society, masculinity in our world is often defined by violence or the capacity for violence and force, or money and what money can buy. I think that frequently the narrow definitions we provide our boys growing up about what it means to be strong, powerful, and admired as a man seep into how we think about public policy and how we organise our societies. Often, it's a stunted view, and part of what we have to do is to expand our notions of manhood and power to include ideas of providing people with health care, caring for children, and being good stewards of the environment. That's what men do now – instead of going to war, making lots of money, and telling other people what to do.*"

**Substantial discussion about the impact of the gender binary of masculinity and femininity deserves chapters in their own right. I encourage you to seek out the voices of gender diverse and trans people especially. In the Resources section, I've recommended brilliant books written by people with lived experience of this. In the context of this book, it's largely about the damage wielded by hetero-normative ideals of masculinity and much of (but not all) the discussion about 'men' refers to cisgender men.

Central Pillars of Modern Fatherhood

In the following chapters, I've divided up the key themes from the Spunk Survey and analysis of some of the hundreds of podcast interviews I've had with men who are fathers. These form the central pillars of modern fatherhood as I've come to identify them – the core set of narratives that modern fathers face.

These central pillars form the backbone of Father Stunter Culture and as we explore and debunk them further, I hope to help you (and I'll be honest, myself) answer how men can find a more authentic and fulfilled identity in being a father and how to find a new way of relating to your **SPUNK**.

FATHERS WITH SPUNK DO

"I've witnessed increasing frustration from men that businesses and organisations don't take it seriously that men want to be more active and involved fathers – which results in a lack or loss of flexible working arrangements for dads. Organisations tend to be run by more senior men, who base their ideas of work on their own experiences, and that's generally based on the traditional gender norms – men go to work and women take care of the children. As we start to see more of a generational shift in leadership roles, people will begin thinking about flexible working in different terms – from the perspective of fathers and their role, their needs, as parents and within the home. We're in completely unchartered territory right now, with the impact of the COVID-19 pandemic. With more men working from home, they've got extra time – from not having to commute, for example. Men are typically very good at taking on the 'hero' stuff with their kids. That narrative of *'oh, daddy's home just in time for bath time'*. I think now it's about understanding the domestic pressures. I don't think enough men fully understand the concept of mental load. Now they're beginning to."

IAN DINWIDDY, Founder of Inspiring Dads

"There's no specific way to be a hands-on dad – you don't have to be the person who's changing nappies all the time or be the person who's doing X job or Y job. I think being a hands-on dad is about being involved in your child's upbringing from before they're even born. Yes, you can change nappies. Yes, you can take them to dance or the gym. Yes, you can cook meals for them. All those things can be done, but those things aren't necessarily about creating a relationship with your child – an individual relationship with them that's unique to you and them. It's about growing that relationship every day. It doesn't matter whether you're with them or not. You can FaceTime, you can send them a text message if they're old enough. That way, they can come to you, they can talk to you, you can talk to them about all the different aspects of parenting and growing up as a child. It's about the relationship you create."

NIGEL CLARKE, TV Presenter and
Founder of Dadvengers

"When you initially set up a business, you don't look for balance because there's no such thing when you're starting. The idea is to build balance, build success, so you can have that balance when the timing is right, and the business is mature enough. I feel like I've managed to achieve that now, but it wasn't easy and it meant my wife taking on more of a traditional role within the home and with parenting. It's never easy. I try to start and finish work at reasonable hours and be more involved, but my brain is always thinking; I'm on my phone, researching, and replying to emails. I know I could do more, and my wife is brilliant – I wouldn't be able to do this without her. I could do more to be more hands-on with the children. While I have a better sense of balance, it's something I'm always striving for."

YING TAN, Founder and Serial Entrepreneur

"There have been times where people come up to me if I'm out with my kids, and they'll make statements like, *'Oh, look, you've got your kids today. That's so great you're spending time with them'*. I appreciate where they're coming from because it's generally a good place, but it also rubs me the wrong way because it's such an outdated perspective. I'm a full-time father to my three children, and it's made me realise it shouldn't be like this. There should be two of us doing this – together. People make assumptions based on gender, and we all do it, but it sucks. Being a single father has given me this perspective I didn't have before, around the inequities in expectations between mothers and fathers. Fathers get applauded for doing the minimum – just *being* around our kids, for example. But it shouldn't be like this. We shouldn't reward such a low bar for parenting."

ROB GORSKI, CEO The Autism Dad, LLC

During the School for Fathers podcast interviews, I've heard men describe the contours of their fatherhood in a multitude of ways. Many guests continue to reflect on their shortcomings and talk equally about the gap between fathering as it is for them and how they'd like it to be. I am used to hearing fathers take ownership of their part in how things are, albeit a few lay the reasons for life's turbulence at the feet of feminists or as a result of individual women's actions, often an ex-partner/wife. Most cover how they're making sense of what I'll label paternal ideologies, and they let me in on their paternal practices. The vast majority critique the ultra-limited standards of 'good fathering'.

They've shown time and again how their experiences vary across race, class, and family structure. Yet, they're lumped homogeneously, firstly as men and secondly into chunky subgroups. Whether that's as, for example, Black (presumed absent) fathers, White work-shy or White workaholic dads, or 'gay' fathers (as if sexual orientation affects the ability to raise children lovingly). Intersections of class, sexuality, and other social locations provide insight into why some fathers appear to be reticent to embrace normative paternal practices, like being so-called 'hands on' with their children.

Being 'hands on' has always sounded weird to me; it reminds me of spanking, a culturally controversial (and in some places) illegal parental practice, given it's proven to be detrimental to child safety and development[1]. I've also wondered what the opposite of hands-on is, akin to the opposite of love not being hate but rather indifference. So, I looked this up, and hands-off equates to impersonal. Strange, huh?!

The option for hands-off, impersonal fathering appears to be available, should men choose this. Surely the antithesis of hands-on, involved fatherhood couldn't be hands-off, impersonal fathers, could it?

But, let's be honest, it can, and all too often is.

I'd like to offer two compelling reasons that strike me for why hands-off fatherhood is possible and condoned. These two reasons don't include the shouts from off-stage crowds saying, "*it's obvious Danusia, it's because women are doing all the work*". Feminist as I am, that's not where I'm pointing, though; *yes*, mothers today still take the lion's share of child-raising. But as Jordan Shapiro reminds us[2], "*Leaving fathers out of the current media narrative normalises the inequity of household care labour, which is not only a misogyny problem but also stigmatises the dads who are trying to do the right thing.*"

Let's muse backward.

Reason One

Few mammalian dads invest as much time nurturing and raising their offspring – or even the children of others – compared to human fathers. A fascinating area of evolutionary academic study has formed around the ways human fathers evolved into their highly invested role in ways almost all other mammals have not. But the role of fathers varies widely between cultures.

"*If you look at other mammalian species, fathers tend to do nothing but provide sperm,*" says Rebecca Sear[3], an evolutionary demographer and anthropologist at the London School of Hygiene and Tropical Medicine. Even among apes, our closest relatives, fathers tend to do little, which affects frequency between pregnancies. For instance, orangutans tend to wait six to eight years between offspring, as mothers shoulder the infant raising. However, our human strategy around this has been described as "*part of the evolutionary success story of humans*" as human mothers historically were able to gather help from kin, including fathers. Shortened gestation periods and a heightened need to look beyond same-sex support meant mothers looked to the person who was as genetically invested in her (or their) child as she was. This was, of course, the father[3]: "*Without dad's input, the threat to the survival of his child, and hence his genetic heritage, was such that, on balance, it made sense to stick around. Dad was incentivised to commit to one female and one family while rejecting those potential matings with other females, where his paternity was less well-assured.*"

Renouncing multiple matings with multiple females simultaneously (in large part) means men's focus on one mate with a commitment to offspring with her is possible.

On top of this unusual evolutionary pathway to human fatherhood, in comparison to other mammals, there have been studies showing changes in testosterone levels meaning human fathers mirror hormonal and brain changes seen in new mothers. "*Irreversible reductions in testosterone and changes in oxytocin levels prepare a man to be a sensitive and responsive father,*" Anna Machin tells us[4]. However, there are contradictory reports that testosterone levels creep back upwards as children grow. This hormonal mechanism appears to encourage fatherly behaviour accounting for human fathers attention to their offspring. Despite these discoveries, it's clear fatherhood in humans is pretty variable[4]. Not all dads are devoted or even present.

Acknowledging the unusual nature of human

males' involvement with their children and hormonal and brain changes does make a difference to understanding human fathers. More so, I believe a general primal undercurrent of a long-held belief that whisper-shouts "*males don't usually do this, you know*" allows the idea of a low bar of involvement to persist. Human males have evolved to be more attentive to their offspring – and other children they choose to care for – and it's clear human fathers ARE unusual in their attention to their children. But the resonance of this low bar of involvement narrative ripples on.

Reason Two

I'd never confronted the idea that, until not too long ago, human males didn't have any assurance a child was genetically theirs. In an extraordinary book, *Paternity: The Elusive Quest for the Father*[5], Nara Milanich breaks down the history of paternity and how we came to think about it the way we do now. Scientifically, DNA testing is considered relatively recent as it was only in the 1980s the technology known as DNA fingerprinting emerged to allow us to say with a very high degree of probability that a given individual is the father or mother of another individual. And only since the 1990s have these technologies become commercialised in an industry that's experienced exponential growth in just the last few years.

From the 1920s, scientists and lawyers became excited about the idea that scientific proof of paternity was possible, even desirable. Undoubtedly, it could serve an important social function to know who the biological father was. Previously, for example, in the nineteenth century, paternity was often defined in social terms and not in biological terms. Think here of how many legal systems automatically defined husbands as the fathers of their wives' children, even if evidence suggested the husband could not be the father. This was a social definition of paternity as opposed to a biological one.

Interestingly, Milanich shares[5], "*the way we think about paternity is very different from the way we think about maternity rights and the ways that law and society have historically defined who the father is, is very different from how we understand who the mother is.*" Maternity has been understood as certain because historically, we can observe with our eyes and see this woman is the mother. Of course, the case of oocyte (egg) donation has meant reconsideration about whether an individual who provides genetic material in the form of oocytes is a 'donor' or an 'intended parent'. Sperm donation procedures are regulated by different legal standards as far as I understand it, and most courts would say sperm donors are not fathers. There are a gazillion examples of court cases where biological paternity is deemed not determined by biology but by something social, so it's the will and intent of the man to be the father that endures. Milanich hammers this home, "*we have powerful scientific ideas about biology and biological determinism from the 1920s, but they never displace the older social ideas.*"

The core question of 'who is the father?' is also tied to questions of how fathers behave or how they should behave. Additionally, paternity issues lead us squarely to reflect on who fathers are considered to be: is the 'real' father the one who contributed the sperm or the one who raises the child? How we've come to define the father rests on a related but distinct question, not *who is the father*, but rather, *who do we want him to be*?

This is why in the survey design I didn't ask a simple "*how many children do you have?*" but asked multiple questions that called men to reflect on what constitutes the father they consider themself to be and to whom. I wasn't interested in whether others see them as a father to X or Y – I wanted to hear it from them.

Surprisingly, the whole idea of unknown paternity, or at the very least, ambiguity about who to count as 'being father to' emerged. I received emails asking me to help men choose how many children they are father to. At first, I thought this was a one-off, then a fluke couple of instances, until I received a flurry of men's genuine requests to define what I meant by 'father figure'. And whether stepchildren who were no longer in the man's life (because of a relationship breakdown) were to be counted. Or how some stepfathers found themselves pulled to say they were father to their biological child/ren on the basis their stepchildren already have a biological dad. I was asked, "*So, what counts?*" more times than I ever anticipated. I'd struck a nerve.

Fathers were called to question, *who am I father to?* And, *what denotes real fatherhood as opposed to another kind of relationship?*

One father wrote telling me he is not a "*current father at the moment*", so how many ought he put down in the survey? I enquired about what he meant by 'current', and he said that because his children live across the world, he isn't a current father, but if they were closer geographically, this would mean that he was a current father, from his perspective.

Remember, I was asking fathers for their voices.

The stats in this section about the number of children are messy. Naturally, there are also questions about children that live with you and children that don't, so there's lots of opportunity to cross-check variables. But the truth of men's confusion, as they shared with me privately, created a tough picture to analyse. The results show low non-residency but high contact with more children than anticipated. I had to ask: Are men leaning into a father figure archetype to explain temporary relationships with children? What does the presence of a biological father mean for stepfathers in terms of occupying a father role? If not a father, what is this relationship? In reverse, what if that biological father voices that now a biological child has a stepfather in their life, the biological father is no longer needed? (*Hello child with neither father fully invested in that relationship on account of the other man's presence.*)

What can we learn from these unravellings about who the father *is* and *wants to be*?

Who is a father is contested. It's shifting. And it's fluid. I was left with a general feeling that fathers in this survey weren't always clear about what role they occupy. For some children in their lives, they are clearcut fathers, but biology isn't necessarily the determiner. The younger the children in a man's life, the simpler the picture appeared to be, although adding in a blended family situation blurred the sharp focus. With all this being said, most respondents reported they are father figures (93.6%) to one or two children (60%), with a slightly higher concentration of fathers of daughters (74.1%) than sons (68.1%).

Hands-On Father Involvement

Expectations of fathers have moved beyond being 'hands on' to being emotionally and practically involved fathers in the lives and care of children. But this is complex. Over several decades up to the turn of the millennium, there were substantial increases in the time fathers spend with their kids[6]. These changes reflect the influence of two dominant discourses around father involvement that point to the importance of paternal time input for children's development and wellbeing, plus the benefits of father involvement in promoting gender equality. It seems unbelievable that father involvement is merely defined as father's, "*positive, wide-ranging, and active participation in their children's lives*"[7]. In reverse, we find father's un-involvement as "*negative, narrow and inactive*" and presumably to be avoided.

This bare-bones definition shows the non-specificity of what a father's involvement could be, in other words, the demarcation lines between uninvolved and involved fathers. Fathers are asking, "*what amount of time is involved enough?*" and "*what kinds of involvement make me active?*". Three levels of paternal involvement were proposed more than thirty years ago; Engagement (shared interactions whether in play, caregiving or leisure), Availability (presence and accessibility to a child), and Responsibility (how much a father arranges resources to be available, including planning and organising children's lives)[8].

But in a 2019 research study[9] outlining current trends on father involvement in the UK, London School of Economics academic Ursula Henz proposed the existence of stark differences between fathers according to class. Comparing fathers' overall involvement between the start of the millennium and 2014, she found, "*a stalling of the transformation of the father role and progress towards gender equality in the home in large parts of the population*". This research showed some stability of involvement; however, in 2014, fathers were less likely to provide interactive care and active fathers provided on average fewer minutes of physical care than in 2000. The study identified negative trends of involvement among lower socioeconomic groups of fathers while, "*fathers in managerial and professional occupations consistently having higher participation rates than other fathers*". These findings added to previous research in which Henz found that family time (with both parents involved with child/ren) had decreased.

Additionally, father involvement on weekend days continued to diverge between high and low socio-economic groups. Fundamentally the hoped-for transformation of father involvement has come to something of a halt in the UK.

Yet only a few years later, men's magazine GQ conducted a large-scale State of Man survey[10] of UK readers to celebrate their 30th anniversary. The **number one** aspect of modern masculinity was identified as ***"Being a present father"*** with "*Being strong in a crisis*" closely behind. To sum up where readers were: "*[Men] know the rules aren't what they were, but the new rules have not yet been set.*" Evolving expectations of fatherhood are set within a context of ground shaking shifts.

Our SPUNK Survey results back this up:

- When asked to agree/disagree along a continuum for the statement, "*I am a good father*", over 90% (91.6%) self-reported as a good father.
- When asked if the mother/s of their children think they are a good father, over 80% (83.1%) agreed they think the mother/s of their children believe they're good fathers.

At first glance, men are rating themselves highly

and the downgraded score attributed to the mothers of their children is not vastly different from their opinion of themselves. There's a level of alignment within their sense of being good fathers. Let's take this a step further.

- When asked, "*I am the best father I can be*", more than 60% (62.5%) agreed, but more than 35% (37.5%) somewhat disagreed with the statement.
- When asked if society expects more of mothers than fathers in the role of parent, almost 80% (78.9%) think society expects more from mothers than fathers.
- When asked if they're happy with how fatherhood is viewed by society, over 56% (56.3%) are not happy with the way it is viewed.

As you'd imagine, most men see themselves as good fathers, but in the same breath, men acknowledge mothers face higher expectations than fathers. The vast majority of fathers in this survey felt good about themselves as fathers but know much more is expected of mothers of the same children. Men are saying it like it is.

Now add in this mix that men are unhappy with

the way fatherhood is viewed. Picking this apart, four out of every ten men in this survey were neutral (neither agree nor disagree) with the way society viewed fatherhood, but the rest aren't. They're unhappy. Here's the kicker: **not one** respondent said they 'somewhat agree' or 'extremely agree' they're happy with the way fatherhood is viewed.

Men are happy with their own good fatherhood (mostly, though some know there's room for change), but they're generally unhappy with the way fatherhood is viewed. Does this mean that the model fathers are rating themselves against is one they don't believe in? Or put bluntly, is the model fucked, but within that fucked model, they're rating themselves as doing well?

Or is it more palatable to *(yes)* recognise that societal expectations are far more stringent on mothers but *(oh well)* since fathers are generally pretty okay about their performance as fathers, then (hey ho); *Nothing to see here!*

Dissonance between fathers' unhappiness of how their fatherhood is perceived and their assessment of themselves as good fathers is open to interpretation. Podcast guests are more circumspect about their 'good fatherhood' as they critique versions of fatherhood that insist on a fixed low bar of fathering practice. They often speak about the conundrum of the very opposite for mothers who operate under standards of involvement that centre selflessness and sacrifice. It's worth noting many (if not most) School for Fathers podcast guests hold deep regard for the mothers of their children. And they see that any slippage for mothers from ultra-high standards is perceived by society as heinous. In contrast, anything above the barest of minimal involvement for fathers is socially rewarded.

The evidence of fathers in this research shows how they know they're expected to do less, but at the same time don't like the way fatherhood is viewed by others yet think they're doing a good job. And that, just maybe, "*where we worry more than we ever have, but perhaps not about the things we should really be worrying about; where we worry enough to worry, but not enough to change... [and] our expectations have never been so stretched, but maybe stretched too far.*"[10]

An exploration of involved fatherhood wouldn't be complete without sharing responses to a couple more key questions.

- When asked, "*What do you enjoy the most about being a father?*", there was resounding solidarity of focus. 'Watching' was the most frequently used word in responses. It's worth resting on that one for a second.

Here's a small snapshot of answers:

- "*Watching them grow. Supporting them and doing my best to be a good listener.*"
- "*Watching my children learn things on their own.*"
- "*Watching my kids grow and develop.*"
- "*Watching my daughter learn and copy my wife's mannerisms.*"
- "*Watching them learn and grow and become their own people.*"
- "*Watching their success.*"
- "*Watching them flourish and become wonderfully kind people.*"

There are many positions fathers can take concerning their children, but from these results, it's clear a large part of their enjoyment is in observational/witnessing roles. Responses demonstrate vividly how fathers especially enjoy and value a watching position which is pretty distinct from more active stances. Digging into this further, this WATCHING focus was backed by answers about helping, which begs the question, *helping who?*

Here's a tiny example of these:

- "*Helping with decision making with my children.*"

- *"Helping do activities with my wife. Camping, art, outdoors stuff."*
- *"Helping shape the kids."*

Another question asked the difference between involved and engaged fathers; respondents didn't unanimously agree there was any difference between these categories, and some suggested this was semantics. But respondents who viewed them as different had a lot to say:

- *"I believe the biggest difference is that being involved means you are there as a parent whether you choose to or not, or like it or not. You're still there. Engaged means you choose when you want to be a parent."*
- *"Involved is being there. Engaged brings in emotions too."*
- *"Involved sounds like less effort."*
- *"In all the years I have been commenting on fatherhood issues, this is the first time I have seen involved and engaged father separated! I would say most fathers are involved. I'm certainly not meaning to single myself out as a good example of an engaged father, but I think that best describes my approach. I sort out vaccinations, playdates, dentist appointments, arrange parents' evenings*

and so on. I do a lot of the family kidmin that many men do not engage with."

On a personal note, I was interested in this question because, throughout my interviews with fathers, it seemed to me many were using the terms 'involved' and 'engaged' interchangeably, the same for 'hands-on' and 'present'. But there was something about the term 'engaged' that also seemed to level it up from these other phrases for fathering. The very fact we discern between these terms means there is optionality built-in, which assumes that someone (the mother, typically) is doing all the primary care. I was curious how men would view this and while some feel it's simply semantics, many do see clear distinctions. It was a good call to ask, especially in the context of SPUNK and this book. In my mind, involved fathers don't necessarily have to be emotionally present, but engaged fathers are. I propose that fathers with SPUNK are ENGAGED, elevating Father Stunter notions of 'involved' or 'hands-on' fathering into a new space. As I write, I also can't help wondering what our children would want if we asked them; an involved, present or engaged dad? What significance do these terms hold for them?

These extra layers – 'watching' fathers and engaged

fathering – contain glimpses of the Father Stunter social and cultural clues that might stop fathers from becoming more involved with their children. But of course, the concrete lives and structural conditions of these fathers are not monolithic. What I interpret here is that fathers are making what they can of themselves and their worlds within limits. These are inextricably linked to fixed beliefs about what it takes to be 'real men'. As philosopher Linda Martin Alcoff[11] argues, our complex intersectional identities make a difference because they affect the kinds of experiences we have access to and how we are oriented to perceive and interpret them. Simultaneous locations within social categories (race, gender, education, ability, class, religion, sexual orientation, etc.) differentially pattern subjective experience and access to power and privilege.

In short, restrictive notions of masculinity and the influence of appointed gender orders permeate involved fatherhood daily, and this implicit clash stymies unambiguous engaged fathering. Substantiating credible masculinity while weaving expressions of loving involvement and engagement with children often fall out of sync and enforce rupture in the worlds of men. In the words of one man about to become a father[12], "*There are a lot of questions around masculinity when you are deciding to be a more involved dad because you are taking on more of the mothering role. It's uncharted territory."*

What follows is a short section outlining advice on how to activate the kind of SPUNK needed to disrupt Father Stunter Culture around being an involved/engaged father, enough to make a difference. As philosopher Jean Wahl[13] says, "*Even in our most individual and private consciousness, we are not separated from others.*"

SPUNKY Fathers Don't WATCH. They DO

The data from the research represents a huge disconnect in current fathers' thinking; their children are the centre of their world, and they want to raise future citizens of tomorrow, BUT the part they enjoy most overall about fatherhood is watching and helping.

Hang on?

As we've covered, fathers are often relegated to the sidelines, spectators in the sport of parenthood – whether by choice or by Father Stunters. Perhaps it's not so much that watching and helping is the part fathers **most** enjoy as much as it's the part they've been **unconditionally allowed** to enjoy?

As a society we profess to support involved fathering, this is not reflected in the day-to-day experiences of fathers. Men are not facilitated or empowered to decide to be involved in their child's care. Their experiences at work, as the target for government policies and during their interactions with social and healthcare practitioners, led many to state that policies and best practices were not leading to a change in culture. Society was merely paying 'lip service' to the idea of father involvement[14]. Recent reports[15] of the exclusion of fathers in birthing suites during the pandemic is the epitome of this – men were literally not able to be involved in one of the central moments of becoming a father.

Much of societal views about fathers centre on them watching proudly while someone else is the primary parent. The first step to becoming a father with **SPUNK** is to disrupt this thinking. Here are a few ideas on how to do this:

- **WATCHING needs to switch to DOING**: Spend some time backtracking through your recent activities as a father. How much was spent watching and helping and how much was spent DOING and LEADING? Be honest. No, I mean it – be brutally honest with yourself and see the disconnect. There'll be no equality until you DO the job of less watching, more doing.
- **Decide what ENGAGED means to you:**

Watching and helping does NOT equate to being engaged. And I'm not *just* talking about changing nappies or school drop off here (although these things are to be included). Go deeper; does it include taking a lead on emotional, sexual and relationship education, championing representations of a healthy relationship with your partner, spouse or ex? Don't worry about what anyone else thinks; what does being an engaged father tangibly LOOK and FEEL like to you.

- **CHALLENGE the narrative**: Another moment of unadulterated honesty is required from you; when someone celebrates your activity as a father, how do you respond? You know what I'm talking about, those comments from strangers about how you're *'having quality daddy time'* with the kids simply for taking them to the park (something mum does three out of four weekends in the month, with no such acknowledgement). It's so easy to sit back and feel proud of yourself in these moments, to consider yourself (as 91.6% of survey respondents did) a 'good father'. Fathers with **SPUNK DO** challenge the narrative. Do not bask in the glory of the bare minimum. This is your moment to disrupt the idea that you are a helpmate, a secondary parent. Stand up and be counted as an engaged father.

FATHERS WITH SPUNK SHARE

"The first rule of being a great dad is being a great partner. The word partner means being equal. Many men I speak with tell me they believe they're a great partner because they do whatever their partner tells them; they ask what needs doing and do it. I have to tell them that's not being a great partner – that's being an assistant, a helper. The highest paid jobs in an organisation are in management because they have the burden of setting the agenda, steering the direction – all of that responsibility sits on their shoulders. And that's the role of so many women in the home. I've spoken with men too, who say they struggle to help in the home because women feel unable to step down, but the truth is, we've created this struggle. Outdated gender norms see many households being held hostage by what's referred to as 'maternal gatekeeping'. Women believe they're *meant* to do it all, and it's *meant* to be easy, along with terms like 'maternal instinct' – we keep women pinned in these double binds, and many of them don't turn to their partners and husbands when they need to because they don't feel the equality in the partnership. It's not there in the ways it's needed."

MICHAEL RAY, Solo Dad, Speaker &
Author of *Who Knew?*

"I often talk about work-life balance for men, and a lot of that centres around men having open and honest conversations in order to figure out what makes sense for their individual families. If it makes sense for one of you to be working twelve hours a day and earning the money that allows you to achieve agreed family goals, then it's not wrong – if it's working for you as a family then it's working. What I do encourage people to talk about and work out as much as possible is how they're ensuring that everyone's needs are met. If your partner isn't happy or needs more help, more headspace to work, downtime, time off from the kids – it's about taking a holistic view of how you live your life and how that fits together as a family, as a husband, as a father."

IAN DINWIDDY, Founder of Inspiring Dads

"Parenting plus work plus building our lives once we become parents is something we all struggle with. Struggle is definitely the right word at times, but other times it's more trying to achieve whatever balance is needed for that moment. My partner and I have one child, and we're both conscious of being present rather than working whenever we're with her and both being very hands-on parents. It's a continual loop of asking the questions about who's looking after her or what does she have that she needs to get to? It's an ongoing balance: how do we balance what we need to do as parents, what we want to do as parents? On the flip side, what do we need to do professionally? Not just in terms of bringing in money, whether it's running a business or as an employee, but also what do we want to do professionally and personally? I do think that's the modern-day juggling act. Sometimes we get it right. Sometimes we don't. I don't think we talk about it enough collectively as a society – together as parents, rather than fathers versus mothers."

CHRIS LAMBERT-GORWYN, Founder of the
HCB Collection of companies

"I thought becoming a father would dramatically change my life, and I wouldn't be able to work as much, or I wouldn't be able to go to the gym. I thought it would be a whole big change in life, but I've got a very accommodating fiancé who's amazing. Early on, we figured out a routine that allowed me to be a part of the baby's life but still gave me the balance I needed for my work, the business and going to the gym. I've just been surprised at how lucky I've been to balance running a successful business and not being a shit dad as well. My dad is amazing, and I feel like I've learned a lot from him as a role model. When I was younger, he worked abroad a lot and wasn't around so much, so mainly my mum raised us, but now he's always around. He, my brother and I are all really close. I think I'm just trying to achieve the same. I'm just trying to have that balance of not being a shit dad and not being there, but also growing a really successful business, which is tough, and holding on to some sense of who you are beyond that. I want to maintain some kind of level of continuing to do things that I want to do. It's a huge juggling act."

DAN KNOWLTON, Co-founder & CMO at Knowlton

Part of my wish to explore fatherhood is to shed light on age-old issues that don't seem to disappear, whether as conversations, heated debates or hackneyed storylines. These happen between spouses, friends, colleagues, in the media, comedy sketches and all over. These issues are sites of controversy for people, yet they can unite us because conversations have the opportunity to fundamentally change things. But there must be a willingness to take critical perspectives and recognise places where we're reproducing old gender patterns.

I'm especially talking about **household responsibility and the mundane grunt work of household chores.** About who does what and when, but also who (appears to) own the domain itself: **the domestic sphere.** It's not a sexy topic, and in busy lives, it can feel far less gruelling just to cut corners and do the easiest thing. Turns out this usually means following traditional gendered division of labour with mothers reducing their hours of employment to take on the so-called 'second shift' of running a home and looking after the children. At the same time, fathers maintain or increase their employment hours to manage a reduction in household earnings and additional expenses[1].

Alongside asking fathers about the specifics of time spent with children, it was helpful to investigate laterally. I wanted to know what respondents thought being a father would be like compared to how it's turning out to be. On top of this were questions about differences between 'good' and 'bad' fathering, and as an essential part of this, their perspectives on 'good' and 'bad' mothering:

- When asked, "*In three words, what fatherly role did you imagine you would take?*", respondents used words like **PROVIDER + PROTECTOR + FUN** in this order. These are the roles men imagined they'd fulfil as fathers.
- When asked, "*Which three words describe your actual experience of being a father?*", respondents answered less about their role and more about their experience of fatherhood; the state of themselves within fathering. A different picture emerged. Respondents didn't use the same words, but two themes were evident: **GUIDE + HARD WORK(ER).** The third word was far more variable, but themes were still present, such as **CONFUSION, CRITICISM, SATISFACTION, and PRIDE.** Not one respondent mentioned fun.

What's striking about these results is that imagined fatherly roles match traditional stereotypic old-style fatherhood, but the actual experience of being fathers, for these survey respondents, doesn't follow that trajectory. This is an interesting departure and is in parallel with reports from mothers (albeit not under the same survey conditions) who find a dramatic difference between the romantic myth of motherhood and, "*the hell, the joy, the mess, the treachery, the grief, the ecstasy, the darkness, and the isolation, the desolation and the heart-swelling gloriousness of being a mother.*"[2] The father-provider model in the imagined role appears to be blurring significantly, but as it does an increase in strain and confusion is highlighted as fathers have to find their way in still uncertain territories.

The majority of men in this survey were raised in heteronormative family structures, where fathers were the provider and 'fun' dad, whilst mum was building the domestic infrastructure to raise the kids. So, respondents may be co-crafting family forms and practices away from what's well known. Goodsell and Meldrum report[3] that fathers adopt diverse roles including nurturer, playmate, primary carer, counsellor, teacher and financial provider, while Habib and Lancaster's study[4] placed breadwinner as fifth on their list of fathering roles behind emotional supporter, playmate, caregiver and helper. This research backs the shift from provider to more nurturant roles and somewhat away from playmate.

There are several reasons for the likely mood of respondents in reflecting on their experiences of fatherhood. Two of the core ones being:

Before the onset of COVID-19 and subsequent lockdowns, (some) fathers had been trying to undo generational patterns of uninvolved fatherhood they'd inherited from their own fathers. This isn't to say all men have been focused on this, but it's been a significant focus for many fathers. Here's how one respondent put this, "*There's not a part of me that wants to be like my own father, and he was a 'decent' man. He brought in the money. It wasn't till he was old and almost dead that we got to know each other. I'm giving my kids more.*"

Then there's the impact of pandemic lockdowns and subsequent revisioning of what's possible, or not, in life. A Fathers Network Scotland (FNS) survey[5] on Lockdown Two found adverse effects of nursery and school closures, disruption to work, loss of jobs, working from home, isolation from family and friends, homeschooling, and absence of social time or time for being alone. Navigating family life since March 2020 has been demanding as multiple strains co-exist and leave fathers stretched under pressure.

Results from the FNS survey showed fathers experienced increased time spent on household chores, homeschooling with children and cooking. Within the research, 37% of dads said their current mental health was bad or very bad, and 69% mentioned their well-being deteriorated due to the second lockdown in Feb-March 2021. As I write, we remain in turbulent times as further SARS-CoV-2 variants emerge and restrictions vary worldwide. Life is indelibly changed and 'new normals' are continuously mobile.

Hence, father identity is currently set within unprecedented globally troubling events. And involved fathering is somehow often collapsed into being a 'good father'. Let's take a look at the results from the SPUNK survey.

When asked, "*What do you consider to be good fathering?*", examples of most frequently reported themes include:

Present	Has a good time	Loving	A good role model	Instils discipline	Listening

The nurturer, teacher, guide, and playmate model of father can be seen here, but so are remnants of a disciplinarian boundary-setting style of fatherhood.

These markers of good fatherhood chime with previous data that showed a move from financial provider over to nurturing based fathering. Being a provider hardly even figured in fathers reporting of what they consider a good father to be!

When asked, "*What do you consider to be bad fathering?*", examples of most frequently reported themes include:

Unavailable	Absent	Demands obedience	Disrespectful to women and/or mothers	Present but absent emotionally	Shirks responsibility

It's clear fathers see involvement with their children as good fathering, although physically being there alone is not enough. That's a basic since fathers here denote being an absent father with being a bad one. Interestingly, showing disrespect to women, and mothers of their children, constitutes bad fathering, which I'm guessing links to showing up as that good role model. Extrapolating this further, the older a father is, the less likely he seems to be concerned with issues of respect towards women. This doesn't mean older fathers in this data set were disrespectful; it's that men over fifty-five didn't mention this as a marker of bad fathering.

It was obvious to ask the same questions for mothering:

- When asked, "*What do you consider to be good mothering?*", respondents agreed on these themes:

Selfless	Creates a nurturing home and supportive environment	Focused on family and relationships	Unconditional love	Being there for the children

Entrenched beliefs about what it takes to be a good mother are shown in these results. Whereas it's not difficult to see that men's attitudes towards themselves as fathers have undergone significant change, the same cannot be said for attitudes about mothers. At least, not for the fathers in this survey.

Good motherhood appears to be displayed by sacrificing oneself and focusing on family, relationships, and homemaking. It's as if we're reading about a 1950's family situation. Mothers being fulfilled in their own right is not mentioned, which is explained when we see what bad mothering is viewed as.

- When asked, "*What do you consider to be bad mothering?*", respondents offered these:

Selfish	Distracted with own needs	Not being there emotionally	Working too much	Too liberal with boundaries

Let me introduce you to mothers who have needs of their own. These are the bad mothers who work too much, who don't or won't dedicate their focus to the home, their children and their partner. From these results, it's too hard to tell where the line could be between 'enough' and 'too much' because respondents weren't asked this. In some ways, respondents are doing what they do to discover what constitutes 'enough' in involved fatherhood for themselves, forming arbitrary lines and when these are crossed, they become deficit.

The most crucial aspect here is how most (but not all) respondents appear to judge good mothers against an archaic and fixed model of motherhood. This harps back to days when legend holds that women focused their energy on child-rearing, homemaking and not much else. One respondent mentioned, "*mothers focus away from family is a loss.*"

It could be argued that societal perceptions of positive fatherhood are affected by ongoing resistance to progressive understandings of what it takes to be a good mother. This leads me to question how respondents support their partner's work and/or study. Let's face it; this ought to be skewed given the above:

- When asked, "*How much do you agree with this statement: I support my partner's work or study*", 72.9% of respondents said they "extremely agree".

Here we are, with the majority of fathers supporting women's focus away from children and the domestic. Notably, not one respondent declared himself unsupportive of his partner's work/study. Curious. On the one hand, fathers hold views about motherhood fixed in a time when a woman's primary role was her family. By the same token, fathers also declare themselves supporting their partner's work/study.

- When asked, "*How much do you agree with this statement: My partner feels I support their work or study*", a different pattern emerges. Only 54.2% of respondents believe their partner would say they support their work/study.

This 18.7% gap begs questions that can't be answered here. Could it be that respondents overstate their support of their partner's work because to articulate lack of support might court disapproval? In conversations on the School for Fathers Podcast, fathers *do* talk about the pressures of women's work on the entire family system, but even in this format, it would be difficult to verbalise the wholesale lack of support for a partner's career or study.

The GQ State of Man Report[6] found the behaviour of men in private differs vastly from when they're in female company. The disconnect between how fathers see themselves supporting their partners versus how fathers think their partner perceives their support is significant. It could be that fathers believe mothers don't get how supportive they are OR, given earlier judgements about good mothers not being distracted from family, it's not such a leap to imagine that mothers know these judgements aren't only societal ones but live close to home, in their partner's beliefs.

Allegedly, motherhood completes a woman and in analysing this proposition attention has also been given to the domestic sphere. In the 1970s, Anne Oakley argued in her groundbreaking research on housework that there exists in our culture an ideology that links women's identities to their role as mothers and as keepers of the home. But it was later in her semi-autobiographical account, *Taking it Like a Woman,* she states[7], "*the tension between the interests of the family and the interests of women as individuals has been rising for some two centuries. It is not possible for these interests to be reconciled.*" The tension of what's been called the can-you-have-it-all debate is not only persistent but blindingly White-centric, as a White woman's 'dilemma' between career and children. To peddle the misperception that a woman's ambition takes her away from her rightful place at home tending to her children and spouse and that the career is secondary to domestic gender roles is to speak only to some mothers. As Dionne Powell argues[8], "*there continues to be an uneven playing field that is more uneven the further you are from White male hetero-normative archetypes.*"

The domestic sphere as a woman's rightful place hardly needs any introduction, does it? Outdated as it seems, I'm interested in reverberations of this ideology in relation to modernising fatherhood:

- When asked, "*In your opinion, which statement most accurately describes your spouse/partner's involvement in your children's lives (whether a new or existing partner)*", of all respondents, not even 30% reported their partner taking on more than them. 57% of Fathers self-reported their spouse/partner (new or existing) having *equal* responsibility in their children's

> lives. Which is to say, fathers are saying they are equal co-parents, while less than 30% acknowledge their partners are responsible for more than them.

It may be ungenerous to suggest that respondents award themselves more credit than they deserve in this area. Nevertheless, this data surprised me. Here's why.

As we know, over the last forty years, increasing numbers of women have entered the labour force, and at the same time, men have increased their contributions to household work, albeit not at an equivalent rate; women continue to do at least twice as much unpaid work compared to men across most industrialised countries[9, 10]. There's been loads of talk about how men got a new look at what it takes to keep a household humming during COVID-19. And lots of them did way more housework or childcare tasks as they worked remotely (if they were in a socioeconomic group to be able to work in this way).

Yet, it's hard to accurately discuss contribution to domestic chores since men and women typically disagree on who's doing what or how well home chores are being done. The American Family Survey[11] is completed by around 3000 families, asking who does what, highlighting one of the biggest problems when talking domestics. Men in the American Family Survey state they pay the bills and split household chores 50:50. Women in the survey concur that men do the admin of bills, but they scoff at the idea of the 50:50 chores split. They insist they do at least two-thirds of chores. In other shades of this research, a little less than 60% of fathers say they have *equal* responsibility in their children's lives. Hang on a moment then; what exactly do they consider equal responsibility? Maybe fathers weren't even thinking about domestic chores when answering that survey question.

What else could it be? No, seriously, I'm flummoxed. **Scratches head**

Academics have already established there's an underlying domestic ideology that housework and primary care of children are traditional feminine tasks that could push some women to take most responsibility because this is a way of 'doing gender'[12], providing a marker of feminine identity[13] and a means of expressing love for the family[9]. The domestic is also gender-segregated concerning the domestic tasks men and women do[14]. Men may shy away from typically 'feminine' work, opting for the nonroutine tasks because this affirms their masculine status. Routine housework, by the way, includes tasks like cleaning, laundry, and cooking rather than 'fun' childcare play tasks. If one partner takes on a disproportionate share of onerous and routine housework, it can lead to dissatisfaction, depression, and divorce[15]. Hence, the division of unpaid domestic work impacts the quality of a relationship, but it is far more common for studies to focus on the consequences of mothers engaging in paid work than fathers' involvement at home. Dissecting this involvement is rarely undertaken. We know that economically framed arguments suggest (in heterosexual unions) couples' joint economic welfare is maximised by the higher earner, usually the man. This means women's engagement in the labour market is seen as a threat. And this is perpetuated by social policies, gender inequalities in the labour market, and cultural ideologies about parenting roles, which say preschool children suffer if their mothers work full-time, and 'good fathers' are ones who provide for their children[16].

What's fascinating is that women are more likely to report housework is shared fairly when men are involved in tasks typically considered 'women's work', such as cleaning, cooking, and laundry. Men's perceptions of fairness are also determined by how much they participated in typical 'female' tasks like feeding, bathing, and changing nappies rather than playing with kids, DIY and gardening.

Beyond physical household tasks, mothers are also more likely to assume the mental and emotional labour associated with caring for children[17] and most responsibility for the planning and management of the household[18]. Eyes to the SPUNK Survey once more:

- When asked, "*How many (waking) hours per week do you see your children?*", over 70% of respondents across the dataset said more than 40 hours a week.

These hours are in sharp contrast to results of a Cadburys Heroes survey[19] of 1,000 British parents, which found the average parent spends a mere five hours per week communicating face-to-face with their children. It could be that respondents related the concept of 'watching' to this question, as in their answer to, "*What do you enjoy the most about being a father?*", that we explored in chapter two, or indeed this may be as a direct result of changing family life patterns due to COVID-19. Whatever the reason, this amount of hours is substantially higher than anticipated.

Going deeper into an analysis of daily life was needed: ***what do our fathers self-report doing day-to-day?***

The aim was to explore what fathers from this survey are doing *and* not doing. Compiling a list of everyday parenting tasks took some sifting into twenty-four core activities. Then the survey asked fathers to select the frequency of doing each one. Please know there will always be something missing, and I've no doubt readers will alert me to absences that just don't make sense!

Clear patterns emerged on 1). Tasks fathers self-reported as most often or always doing, 2). Tasks they and their partner do equally, and 3). Tasks they rarely or never do:

Family tasks fathers self-report as most often or always doing:	**Family tasks fathers self-report they and their partner do equally:**	**Family tasks fathers self-report as rarely or never doing:**
• Helping children with their homework • Playing with children • Putting children to bed/checking the children go to bed when they have to • Reading with/to children	• Attending parents' evenings & other school events • Cooking children's meals • Dressing & undressing children/ Monitoring whether children are appropriately dressed • Purchasing of school equipment including sports kits, stationery, lunchboxes	• Arranging medical, dental & other appointments • Administering medicine/monitoring that children take their medicine • Arranging social events for children, e.g., playdates, sleepovers, parties, clubs, etc.

Family tasks fathers self-report as most often or always doing:	Family tasks fathers self-report they and their partner do equally:	Family tasks fathers self-report as rarely or never doing:
	• Tidying up after children or getting them to tidy up after themselves • Taking children on outings • Transporting children from social events • Washing & bathing children/Monitoring that children wash & bathe	• Contact with school & responding to school communications • Disposal of clothes when children outgrow them • Packing & unpacking school bags, lunch boxes, sports kits • Personal care, e.g., head lice, haircuts, cutting nails • Planning & purchasing food for children's meals • Purchasing of clothes • Purchasing children's toiletries & other essentials • Washing & changing children's beds • Washing, drying, ironing & putting away clothes for the children

On this, it's worth noting ethnic and cultural differences do make a difference to participation in household tasks. For instance, a much lower proportion of Indian and Pakistani fathers change nappies regularly than other groups[20].

In short, fathers who ask, '*how can I help?*', imply the job owner is not them! All the above family tasks are acquirable skills; there's no reason fathers can't perform them.

There are two caveats here worth mentioning. The first is around fathers as solo care providers, who simply have no say in when or how they step up to the challenge of taking their share – they simply must. Paternal solo care requires fathers to take on heightened responsibility for anticipating and attending to children's needs as a primary parent. Caring solo develops a 'care competence' for men wherein they build confidence in their caregiving practices. This helps facilitate a shift from a helper-manager dynamic in the family to co-parenting.

The second is around the notion of 'Maternal Gatekeeping'. A member of the School for Mothers Facebook community group, summed up this concept well when she commented: "*My kids, my rules. My husband has no say. I often tell him he's just a sperm donor, and the parenting law and commandments fall to me.*"

If we are to expect fathers to take their share, to step up and actively be engaged in the domestic life of the home in the ways ALL parents say they would like (indeed, are already saying they're doing if we go by the survey data), mothers must be willing to take their hands off ownership of the domestic. Remember, the Father Stunter Culture would have us believe men are incapable of stepping up in this domain. Maternal Gatekeeping is an excellent example of Father Stunters at work. There's something powerful about calling out the litany of comments (whether that be with a woman, partner, wife, mother, other family members, or even your colleagues in the staff kitchen) that serve only to treat men/fathers as not only incapable within the home and childcare but to further perpetuate the BS that women can or should do it all. Allyship is required here.

Parental and Maternal Gatekeeping are concepts I could easily dedicate entire chapters to (and have had many an excellent conversation about within both my podcast series), but for the sake of brevity, we'll leave them here for now.

Ultimately, many fathers rarely flex their nurturing muscles when a mother is nearby. Some might argue nurturing is *not the same* as family chores but, to return to the notion of **engaged fatherhood**, this involves all parts of raising kids. Including household tasks and the emotional labour of everything that comes with managing not only a household but the transformative needs of children as they grow. It's in the daily wear and tear and intimate contact with the needs of children that deep nurturing relationships exist. This is where fathers with **SPUNK** not only share domestic labour but willingly grab hold of their share with both hands.

Fathers with SPUNK Take Their SHARE

I loved when Michael Ray, in our conversation for the SFF podcast, talked about how he challenges men who say they're a great partner because they ask their partner what needs doing and then do it. As he says, "*That's not being a great partner – that's being an assistant*".

When it comes to the domestics, we have this intense clash between the notion that women are 'meant' to 'do it all' and the Father Stunter bullshit that men 'can't' do it. This delightful conundrum is packaged tidily by long-held ideas of appropriate 'feminine' and 'masculine' tasks around the home, wrapped up beautifully with a bright, shiny (sometimes dark) bow of Maternal Gatekeeping.

Put simply, the domestic sphere is NOT a woman's sphere. Domestics are the lens through which we see equality as possible. The next step in rewriting the **SPUNK** script involves ripping open the aforementioned package and fathers grabbing their share of the domestics by the proverbial balls, disrupting the notion this is 'women's work' and focusing on developing the skills that MAKE them equal. Here are a few ideas:

- **STOP being an assistant and STEP UP as a Domestic Partner:** This one's relatively easy. STOP asking your partner *how can I help,* and START being proactive. HOW can you be proactive, you ask? Oh, stop it, please. Open your eyes – take a look around, really, take a good look. See something that needs doing? Good – now do it.
- **Take RESPONSIBILITY for the MUNDANE:** Fathers with SPUNK SHARE the mundane, the nuts and bolts of invested sustained care, the emotional and mental load. The impact of not being responsible – or not claiming responsibility – for these aspects of daily, domestic life is further heightened by narratives perpetuated through Father Stunter Culture of fathers as being infantile and incapable. So, ask yourself: HOW am I currently claiming my responsibility for the mundane and what needs to change?
- **REVIEW your MOST OFTEN, EQUALLY and RARELY tasks**: Head over to the Appendix and use the twenty-four parenting tasks as a starting point. Add in your own. Rate them as we asked our survey respondents, and then take this list to your spouse or partner to review together. Once

they've stopped laughing, sit down and make a plan together for how to address perceived and actual imbalances going forward (this will also help you switch from assistant to Domestic Partner).

FATHERS WITH SPUNK CARE

"My three sisters and I grew up in the late 70s and 80s, and my dad was our primary carer – so I saw firsthand the struggles he went through. He was the only dad in the playground most of the time, and whereas now we have a lot more understanding and compassion, there wasn't so much of that. It was considered a very odd thing. Fast-forward forty-odd years, I was a senior analyst for a media agency, commuting a lot. I'd get home very late at night and be able to put my son to bed if I was lucky. Even then, I wasn't fully present – I still had my phone out, answering client emails. Even I saw that as my role, as the man in the house, to go out and be the provider. When I spent more time with my son on weekends, he struggled because he didn't know, as a three-year-old, who I was. And that was tough. I was faced with the traditional narrative of being the breadwinner or spending more time with my son, which still wasn't seen as the 'done' thing. This made me take a long hard look in the mirror and actively change the way I was living my life. I quit the commute and made a conscious effort to be more present on everything I was doing, from being there on the school runs, organising playdates, to having a complete change in my career that allowed my son to take priority. Both my son and I deserve that."

DAN FLANAGAN, Founder of Dad La Soul

"I'm constantly hearing parenting and care work referred to as 'women's work', and women's work is always undervalued and underpaid. My retort is always, so what you're saying is I'm doing women's work as a solo-parent? And I get the same response of '*well, it's mainly women that do it.*' I question then whether it's more valued and paid when male peers do it? We need to recruit more stakeholders – and by that, I mean more men, more fathers – into the fold than exclude them, so we can start saying parenting and caring is underpaid and undervalued. When we do that, more men will start to say, '*well, hang on; I'm a parent, I'm a carer; what's this about?*' The biggest problem with many of the equality initiatives is they've made it easier for women to work outside of the home while still maintaining responsibility for all the work inside of the home. We've given women the option to go out and work *and* be mothers if they want, but it's tough. There hasn't been a concurrent push for fathers to be able to leave work and take up more responsibility in the home, especially when it comes to parenting."

MICHAEL RAY, Solo Dad, Speaker & Author of *Who Knew?*

"Reflecting on my dad's era, I think there was much less questioned by men and a lot less expected from men. The man's role was clearly defined, in that he was expected to go to work, and there was never a question that the mum wouldn't stay at home. That was such a default setting; there was no question about it. We can now choose if we want to be involved and how much. That's a privilege in itself. We, as fathers, determine the degree to which we want to be involved. And there are so many different ways we can choose to be involved, with family, with children, with work. This choice creates opportunity, but also deep uncertainty in the sense of instability because there isn't a clear-cut path to keep following."

DAVID WILLANS, Founder of BeingDads

In the last chapter, we explored how men with SPUNK take their share in domestic life. I purposefully positioned this central pillar as one where men can take greater ownership without *too* much grief from inhibitory structural policies that may impede how and when they do. In this chapter, I want to pivot away from housework and the domestics to focus on an area that is linked but also distinctly separate; the idea of breadwinners versus what I refer to as **carewinners**.

The traditional concept of 'breadwinner' concentrates on earning as the means of demonstrating that one (typically men) are providing for their family and erases any care elements.

Tweaking this, we can combine notions of financial provision with caring, in a more robust sense, for men to empower themselves as carewinners. Carewinning is an acknowledgement of the importance and equal desirability of both sides of the coin – that men are needed to provide in a multitude of ways for their families. It also starts to open the door on banishing the age-old, Father Stunter excuse that dad brings home the bacon and, therefore, little else is needed from him.

Let's just revisit the domestics for a moment. According to Dan Cassino[1], men especially avoid housework just when you'd think they'd pick up the slack; when they make less than their wives do. What's more, in female-breadwinner households, the greater the income disparity, the less housework the husband/partner does. Cassino speculates being out-earned by women threatens men's masculinity, so they react by doing less housework, a stereotypically feminine task. The only exception to this double-injustice? **Cooking.** The more wives/partners earn, the more time men spend in the kitchen. Cooking has become manly in a way that pushing a vacuum about has not, partly because of the specialised equipment and techniques involved, but also because it's become a leisure activity rather than a chore. Meanwhile, Cassino has high hopes that housework will similarly become degendered. Maybe one day, hey?

In the research for SPUNK, I followed a hunch triggered from episodes on the School for Fathers Podcast. I was hearing men talk about feeling mocked, and I wanted to know more:

When asked, "*Do you ever feel mocked or ridiculed as a father?*", 28% of respondents answered 'Yes'. This might seem like a lowish figure at first but let me ask, if thirty men out of a hundred in a room felt mocked or ridiculed, would you see that as something to shrug off? I doubt it. To paint this picture for you, here are some excerpts from responses:

Fathers spoke of the media's treatment of them:

- "*The media treats fathers like kids – incapable, silly and irresponsible. We're portrayed as hapless or deadbeat.*"
- "*Fathers are treated as idiots in the media.*"
- "*I'm sick of being the butt of jokes in the media.*"

Fathers mentioned being ridiculed by other men:

- "*When I told some male coworkers I was going to take paternity leave; I was mocked quite a bit. I heard comments like, 'raising kids is women's work' or 'why are you taking maternity leave?'*"
- "*Mates laughed at me for not doing a 'real' job.*"
- "*I was a stay at home father, which I feel was mocked as generally not the norm. Friends didn't know how to treat me anymore.*"

Fathers shared how women and mothers of their children mock them:

- *"I've been mocked from women who assume fathers are stupid and incapable of looking after their children and that just because they are mothers, their way is right."*
- *"Prime example would be the time I was bottle feeding my youngest daughter in a cafe. A woman approached me, lifted her out of my arms and told everyone present I was 'babysitting.' That was an, erm, an interesting moment! More interesting still was the fact her adult daughter was with her. She looked on, quite shocked, and informed her mother I was 'just being a dad'."*
- *"Women make fun of men as if we're children. They patronise our abilities, but it's sad that other men play this to avoid having to do anything."*
- *"I was banned from assisting my daughter backstage at her ballet concert and have been abused for using parents' rooms. Some of the comments are patronising."*

It would be easy, and perhaps not totally unfair, to explain this as a straightforward case of men getting a taste of their own medicine (ouch). But the micro tsunami sharing of ridicule examples suggests something more complicated is going on. There are surely considerable benefits to being treated as 'one of the kids' and colluding with being mothered by women who simultaneously hold a low bar for partners while bigging every little thing up.

Infantilisation of men by women acts to uphold their dominant position over a sphere they've been assigned power historically within – the private space of caring for children. Letting go of a compulsion to control power and standards in the domestic space and with childcare seems a no brainer. However, the social reality is women have historically been left out of the public sphere and still fight for recognition and equality within it, leaving some wielding what power they can muster in the private. This is not to underplay or discount one of the most alarming consequences of the pandemic and (temporary) lockdown policies in many countries; the drastic increase in the domestic violence of men against their partners[2].

Interestingly, the vast majority of respondents' comments were about women's ridicule and mocking. Western cultural expectations of women, especially mothers, reiterate several fixed characteristics. For example, being selfless and unconditionally loving. Indeed, the SPUNK Survey results here stress this portrayal of the 'good mother'. These notions may significantly inform the reception of critical comments about fatherhood. Participatory fathers are typically regarded as exceptional, even heroic, so it must be something of a shock to be at the receiving end of ingratitude rather than congratulations. In the main, these women are positioned as bad human beings who refuse to carry out what is expected of them: caring, maternal behaviour. What it is to be a father is changing and men are caught betwixt. We need to keep remembering human vulnerability and fragility. The privileging of masculinity within patriarchy still means men are hurt by and deeply wounded within the destructive workings of patriarchy. Patriarchal culture eats its own. Importantly, an emphasis on heteropatriarchy essentialises the claim that all men benefit from it, shifting attention from the disproportional distribution of benefits. The brutal truth is men are not all equally oppressors since they gain unequally from patriarchy due to particular lived combinations of race, gender, sexuality, and class.

With that being said, let's turn to the concept of breadwinner versus carewinner in more detail, particularly how scholars suggest that earning an income is not a sufficient condition for being defined as a breadwinner[3].

Many studies have examined the connection between fathering and breadwinning, and all agree there's evidence of changing ideals and practices[4]. It's said modern fathers want to be approachable providers who provide economic provision and emotional and social support, while also nurturing and bringing up kids. Before we go further, there are many versions of male breadwinning (men's primary responsibility for earning an income for the family) and universal breadwinning (both partners are fully engaged in the labour market, but income distribution is unclear). There's broad agreement that glorifying breadwinner masculinity is problematic because it relies on a gendered, heteronormative view of the traditional nuclear family as a heterosexual couple with children[5]. Let's revisit the SPUNK Survey data on this:

- When asked, "*Please select your partner's employment status (paid or voluntary*", 62.5% of respondents have a partner who is employed full-time, which is lower than the OECD full-time rates recorded in 2019[6]. The results here include the US and are almost certainly affected by COVID-19.
- When asked, "*On a scale of 1–10, in your opinion, how much of a breadwinner do you feel you are?*" and "*On a scale of 1–10, in your opinion, how much of a caregiver do you feel you are?*", overall respondents associated being **more** breadwinner than caregiver.

Responses were extended across caregiver segments but were intensively bunched within the breadwinner options. Although there's dedication to caregiving as an identity for fathers, breadwinner was the priority. But what's interesting is that underneath the breadwinner construct is *taking care of family stability* which equates to caregiving. Although this survey did not ask directly about the meanings behind these terms, it was possible to cross-match answers from open text box input to see that, for many men, caregiving includes being a breadwinner.

In some respects, this would make sense since, anecdotally, fathers talk about being a breadwinner as a way of showing that they *care about* not only *care for* their families. I propose the creation of a separate category that acknowledges the multiplicity of positive intent of fathers as they support and love their families. **Carewinner** offers the opportunity to legitimise the father's commitment to caring as well as breadwinning.

While this linguistic switch might help fathers, it won't change underlying beliefs. But language <u>is</u> a signifier of power for "*when we speak,*" Blanchot[7] says, "*we gain control.*"

When asked, "*Please indicate how much you agree with: Being a father is harder than being at work*", almost 70% (69%) of respondents felt being a father is harder than being at work.

Is it really surprising to learn that fatherhood is harder than work? (Many) fathers are experiencing multi-role dissonance and exhaustion in unrelenting times.

When asked, "*What do you consider is the biggest barrier to being a good father?*", respondents offered many insights. Here is a snapshot of responses:

- "*Outdated ideas of masculinity.*"
- "*Knowing what I'm meant to be doing.*"
- "*Societal beliefs about fathers.*"
- "*Men who don't support equality as carers.*"
- "*View of fathers as masculine machines, not humans.*"
- "*Stress at work. Stress at home.*"
- "*Having the confidence to fight for my child's interests against their mum.*"
- "*Being headstrong on topics that we ought to be more open-minded on.*"
- "*Society's view of fathers' secondary role as parents.*"

That last one is telling. Thinking back to Father Stunter Culture and the emergence of guides seeking to degender parenting terms, you'll remember that a recommended term for father was secondary biological parent.

Everyday work takes so much energy that fathers (and mothers) can sometimes feel too tired to participate in family life, contributing to work-family conflict. Compartmentalising work and family in an effort to cope with excessive demands from both domains is a common tactic for fathers. Fatigue from work is a negative spillover, and sometimes fathers enact what LaRossa[8] calls, "*imitated involvement of fatherhood conduct*", that is, a situation where the father tries to look as if he is taking care of the children (to meet the expectations of fatherhood) but is actually watching television or some such activity.

One common rationalisation for the typically limited time given to children is for working fathers to highlight the importance of quality over quantity time. In this narrative, men value short-term positive experiences (playtime, fun activities) over daily, continual childcare and domestic tasks. This chimes with the idea of "*the best bits of fatherhood*" that values erm, the best bits of fatherhood, e.g., the most enjoyable bits of being a father[9]. Mundane caregiving versus play-based care is a gendered concept – and if you remember, playmate was one of the reported roles[10] fathers adopt. But this is far more than 'daddy gets the fun bits of parenting and mummy gets all the crap'. Of course, it could be argued this regularly reproduces the same old sexist labour disparities at home.

Evolutionary anthropologist Anna Machin[11] argues rough and tumble play with fathers has evolved as crucial to the father-child bond and for the child's development. Rough and tumble is a specific form of play characterised by highly physical play with lots of throwing up in the air, jumping about and tickling, accompanied by loud shouts and laughter. Her research found this form of play is a time-efficient way to get hits of neurochemicals required for a robust bond. This is especially important for fathers who spend more of their waking hours at work than in close contact with their children. How do we know rough and tumble play helps develop father-child bonds? As Machin tells us, "*hormonal analysis has shown that, when it comes to interacting with each other, fathers and children get their peaks in oxytocin, indicating increased reward, from playing together. The corresponding peak for mothers and babies is when they are being affectionate.*" Boisterous play, for Machin, holds the key to teaching children about social interaction and resilience, understanding reciprocity and turn-taking, assessing risk and dealing with challenges as children take bigger and bigger physical risks.

In the horrible tradeoff between long hours, economic provision for the family and raising children, this aspect of father-child relationships can be dismissed as the 'fun' side of being a parent. When this is the dominant, or only, form of interaction devoid of participation in mundane low-status household tasks, an imbalance of responsibility is a reasonable assessment of the situation. Unless culturally that's not the case, or where traditional gendered sole breadwinner roles are agreed and performed in which fathers assume sole responsibility to secure their families subsistence. From this vantage point, any participation in childcare, including play, is viewed as praiseworthy.

No matter the chosen breadwinning model, contemporary Europeans (94%) agree men ought to take as much responsibility for home and children as women[12]. As a relevant aside:

When asked, "*Please select your employment status (paid or voluntary)*" and given options, the breakdown was as follows:

– 6.3% of respondents are stay at home fathers
– 60.9% of respondents are employed full time

- 23.4% of respondents are self-employed
- 9.4% of respondents are 'Other', the majority of whom are retired

Social policies have the *potential* to offer employed fathers the chance to participate more in family life while retaining job security. One policy to aid this is paternity leave, defined as an entitlement for fathers that enables them to take a short period of paid time off work immediately following the birth of a child, often associated with providing help and support to the mother. The focus on supporting and helping mothers is, in part, problematic. Undeniably, the birth of a baby brings the need to support the mother (and other children, where appropriate). The invisibility of men starts early in the perinatal period and continues into postnatal time and onwards. Then there's also parental leave, a longer period of paid or unpaid leave from work, designed to provide a parent with the chance to care for a young child – this is separate from paternity and maternity leave. Next, we have (if you're lucky) flexible work arrangements where employees have some control around how, when, and where they carry out their work, including part-time work, compressed work schedules, parental leave, flexible start and finish times, taking a leave of absence, and working from home[13].

The International Network on Leave Policies and Research[14] annually publish information on European fathers' rights to paternity and parental leaves and their use of these rights. The 2021 report covers forty-seven countries and shows many fathers pass up the opportunity to take paternity and parental leave, despite the fact (in some countries) it is often well-paid. Let's check results from the SPUNK Survey on the matter of paternity leave.

When asked, "*Did you take paternity leave when your child/children were born?*", over half of the men (55.4%) took paternity leave for their children. Those who did not take paternity leave were asked for reasons, which were cited as:

- "*My wife was there.*"
- "*My work has no paternal leave options.*"
- "*I worked from home.*"

Paternity leave remains an outlier in the US (many survey respondents for this book reside in the US), and it's the only developed nation that doesn't have a law mandating paid leave for parents. For workers, access to paid leave is typically determined by an employer's benefits package. Even among Fortune 500 companies, parental leave isn't a given. About seven in ten Fortune 500 companies offer some sort of paid leave for new parents, but fathers are generally considered secondary to mothers (there's that Father Stunter notion of secondary once again). Japan has some of the best paternity leave on offer in the Organisation for Economic Co-operation and Development (OECD), but sadly, only an estimated 6% of men take any leave.

Sociology professor Richard Petts[15] asks, "*If men are not supposed to take leave, who cares for the child in a gay couple?*" He notes, "*These gender norms are so ingrained and prevalent that we as a society have a hard time dealing with individuals who don't strictly adhere to these traditional gender norms.*" Not only this, the current structure of paternity leave exacerbates family inequalities, as more advantaged families are more likely to have access to (and the ability to take) paternity leave and its related benefits. Connections between inequality and parenting practice suggest a meaningful way for policy to address an increasing social problem trend. In the UK, if couples are lucky enough to qualify for parental leave, uptake will remain low unless the father works for one of the few progressive companies that offer enhanced pay for all parents. Aviva, for instance, offers its UK staff the right to a year off work, including twenty-six weeks on full pay, regardless of their sex after they have a baby. In 2020, 99% of new fathers at the company took parental leave, with 84% taking at least six months – three weeks more, on average, than in 2018.

Danny Harmer[16], Chief People Officer at Aviva, advises: "*The thing about equal parental leave is that it just changes the conversation about who is the primary and secondary carer; it changes the mindset around hiring. It nudges people away from some of the bias.*"

When asked, "*How often are you able to work flexible hours?*", 75% of respondents said they *are able* to work flexibly, although only a small percentage of them take advantage of this. Significantly, 16.1% find themselves needing to take time off from work regularly (once a week) for children or parenting responsibilities.

For the last six years, Flex Appeal has been lobbying the government hard and campaigning on the streets of London, Manchester, Cardiff, Bristol and Edinburgh. Anna Whitehouse, Founder of Mother Pukka and Flex Appeal, shares[17]: "*Flexible working has never been about location, it's always been about inclusion. It's about including talent. Talent with caring responsibilities, talent living with disabilities. People who are looking to work in a human – or even humane – way that's ultimately good for business. And now we can prove that it's good for business. That there's a direct link between flexibility and profitability. That an uptake in flexible working will boost the UK economy, too. If we want to 'Build Back Better', now is the time for businesses to use flexible working as the foundation."*

Prior to the COVID-19 pandemic and subsequent lockdown policies, scholars argued flexible working did little to disrupt the gender-normative assumptions or the power dynamics within households that determine who should be responsible for housework and childcare. Rather, flexible working could allow heterosexual couples to continue to "*do gender*"[18] and maintain or increase the traditional division of labour within households. However, the large-scale use of homeworking during the pandemic and how it was introduced changed the perception of workers and managers toward flexible working. Flexible working is <u>not</u> simply about working from home – it can refer to, "*working patterns, workload, workplace or life events*" and "*as any way of working that suits an employee's needs, for example, having flexible start and finish times.*"[18]

It's possible to see shifting perceptions of the "*flexibility stigma*" (negative perceptions toward workers who work flexibly for family purposes[19]) as well as the "*femininity stigma*" (flexible working for care purposes makes men deviate away from both ideal worker image and the male breadwinner image[20]). Flexibility stigma was prominent in the UK before the pandemic, with almost one-third of the population believing flexible working negatively impacts one's career[21]. It's likely respondents in this survey didn't take up the possibility of flexible working, even when their family circumstances needed it, because of flexibility and femininity stigma. Expanding flexible working for all workers can help remove some of the existing stigma against flexible working and the career penalty attached by making it a norm rather than the exception. Flexible working alone does not sufficiently disrupt gender-normative views of who is responsible for breadwinning and who is responsible for caregiving. Parental leave supporting fathers' involvement in childcare throughout a child's life, not just in the early years, is crucial to changing societal norms around gender roles.

Additionally, working cultures of a masculine ideal worker norm[18] mean long working hours are considered a sign of workers performance, commitment, and motivation. Flexible working and its blurring of boundaries between work and family life can lead to encroachment of work on other spheres of life and increase competition among workers, where workers end up working everywhere and all the time. To ward against potential exploitation of the workforce, serious consideration has to be given to tackling insidious long work hour culture through reforms such as the introduction of a four-day week. Moving from fixed notions of breadwinning to care-winning, set within endorsed contexts of flexible work, would potentially begin to undo some of the backward harm caused by the pandemic to gender inequality.

Stepping up into and claiming the identity of carewinner is a vital step for fathers with **SPUNK** – but it's not an easy one. Father Stunter culture and the additional structures at play that continually sees fathers demoted to secondary when it comes to all things care in relation to their children means this will take work. Challenging, yes, but not impossible.

As the SPUNK Survey data suggests, fathers already include concepts of care within the bread-winner identity. I believe that by moving to support a reframing of fathers from breadwinners to care-winners – thereby empowering men to further take ownership of the care of and caring for their children – we will rapidly see this central pillar crumble.

Fathers with SPUNK are CAREWINNERS

It's all well and good fathers *thinking* that being a

breadwinner includes ideas of care, but where are the practicalities to support fathers to *actually* get involved with care? Structural change is required urgently, and if ever there was a time to do it, now is it (with thanks for the most part to the forced set of circumstances we find ourselves navigating owing to COVID-19). With all this talk of a return to normal, I would argue our pre-pandemic lived experiences of 'normal' weren't serving anyone, least of all fathers in workplaces.

In reality, this means more support for working fathers (there's a term you don't hear often), public policy and institutions: Paid family leave, flexible work arrangements and the **FULL** integration of fathers into prenatal and postnatal care.

Practically, I can't sum up what this could or should look like more effectively than Flex Appeals 2021 Flexonomics Report[17]. Here are my key takeaways from their recommendations, but I highly recommend (insist) you read the full report:

- **FLEXIBLE working is MORE than HOME working:** It doesn't take a rocket scientist to know this, and yet it still doesn't appear to be widely accepted that the two are distinct from each other. So, I encourage you to ask, HOW do we change this? Or, more precisely, what are YOU going to do about this? How can we work collectively to reshape work patterns? What ACTIONS are involved? Who do you need to collaborate and speak with – whether at a community level or within your workplace – OR are you the person responsible for steering these changes in your organisation? Have you done this? And if not, why not? Only by deciding that the change STARTS with you and taking direct ACTION can this narrative change.

- **Key organisations need to LEAD by example:** This means across all phases of a business – from recruitment through to annual reviews and HR policy updates. The government should consider going further in communicating to businesses the benefits of flexible working, adopting flexible working as the default for the civil service and government departments, or promoting those organisations that do provide robust, flexible opportunities. Remembering that fathers in the SPUNK Survey said they enjoyed the 'watching' aspects of fatherhood, it's important not to let this seep outwards. Fathers with SPUNK **DO**; don't wait around expecting someone else to do this on behalf of fathers – show leadership.

- **FLEXIBILITY for ALL:** In recognising that flexible working is more than homeworking, the report highlights how even the traditionally 'hard-to-flex sectors' can embrace flexibility. The report cites the example of how construction workers can take advantage of self-rostering; reflecting on other industries (especially male-dominated industries where this will be trickier), we have to ask – how can this change? What are the proactive solutions, and how do we voice our needs in this respect in change driven ways?

The more this idea of fathers stepping up centre stage on the playing field and away from the side-lines spreads across pockets of society, the more we can normalise their place as carewinners and the more we empower fathers to embrace a new expectation of who they are as carers – one I know they are raring to claim.

Fathers with **SPUNK** *are* carewinners, and while that does mean standing up as a carer, in all sense of the word, without significant shifts in how they are currently treated, represented and expected to step up as carewinners, many will continue to struggle.

FATHERS WITH SPUNK FEEL

"Something I've learned, particularly through all the conversations I've been having with other dads, is that it's so important to be able to find the level of comfort that's required for the context of the conversations you need to be having with your children. The velocity of how things are changing is quicker than dad's ability to shift to how we relate to our children. If we don't have that baseline of an open mind in this willingness to learn, to feel, to help other dads through listening to their perspectives, respecting them and helping each other – it's going to be very difficult. None of us are perfect. We make mistakes. And we need to accept that as part of the richness of the relationship we can build with our children."

TIM TAYLOR, Host of The Father Daughter Dance Podcast

"Those of us who have the insight and life experience need to model positive behaviours for other men. We need to help each other get better at learning how to be in touch with our feelings and that it's okay to express ourselves. It's okay to go to counselling, seek help for our mental health, and focus on our self-care needs. It doesn't surprise me that a lot of media around self-care is focused on mothers, but there's very little for fathers. We need to prioritise these things for ourselves too. When we do right by ourselves, we do right by our kids, and we set ourselves up to raise good little humans, ones who will be positive people within society, regardless of the challenges they may live through. Everybody contributes. Everybody brings light to the world – that includes dads. It's our job to help that happen and guide our kids. They need us, but unfortunately, it seems there are a lot of dads that become disconnected. I wish that weren't the case, but it's an ongoing issue we need to work on."

ROB GORSKI, CEO The Autism Dad, LLC

"From the time we're born, from the time we begin to understand language in Western culture, we're told what it is to be a man. We receive all sorts of messages about what it is to be a man, about manhood and masculinity. But we're never told explicitly about what it is to be an adult – how to wear and carry adult responsibility, not as a duty, obligation or burden. There's nothing wrong with duty, nor is there anything wrong with obligation, but there's a difference with responsibility. To understand that part of it is understanding, as adults, we *get* to be responsible for ourselves. We *get* to be responsible for our worlds."

KEN MOSSMAN, Entrepreneur and Executive Coach

"The traditional role for men, as partners and parents, has always been focused on being a financial provider. I've realised that the emotional support side of things is equally as important – both providing emotional support and receiving emotional support. Suicide rates are highest for men over the age of forty-five in the UK, and you realise the bottom line is men don't talk. Men neglect the emotional support they need to live up to the roles they're expected to fulfil."

DAN FLANAGAN, Founder of Dad La Soul

Over time, masculinities evolve. In particular, the degree to which aspects of the fatherhood role are valued or encouraged is changing. As discussed, the 'hybridisation' of fatherhood involves an expansion of nurturing and emotional bonding – traditionally seen as more feminine aspects of parenthood – in modern constructs of idealised manhood.

We know these elements are not new. They represent a shift in emphasis compared to historical constructs of masculinity which focused on the father's obligations as provider and disciplinarian. Fatherly affection was primarily demonstrated through pragmatic care – economic provision and labour. Societal pressures compel(led) men to act according to stereotypical gender models of masculinity. For example, they are still expected to be rational, brave, aggressive and emotionless beings and perform 'involvement' as strong-sensitive nurturers and role models for future citizens. Taken collectively, the modern cultural model of fatherhood is complicated and contradictory.

Moving forward with the concept of carewinners, I want to take this further and explore how fathers with SPUNK evolve to take concepts of care beyond everyday needs and into the realm of tending to emotionality – both theirs and their children.

A conceptualisation of fatherhood in relation to masculine emotionality was offered by Esther Dermott[1], who coined the term 'intimate fathering'. This form of fathering values close bonding through repeated personal communication and self-disclosure. Unlike breadwinners or providers, intimate fathers are focused on preserving the quality of the emotional relationship they share with their children and emphasise positive displays of affection, which helps them build a close and long-lasting bond with their children. Intimate fathering happens in the context of an increased lack of reliance on the durability of other intimate relationships, and these parent-child relationships are considered more durable than marriage/partnership in an age of fluid relating and fluid loving[2].

It's assumed intimate fathers reject the dominant narrative of traditional fatherhood, characterised by breadwinning, and construct their intimate role in new ways and through trial and error. With no (common) definition of this new model of intimate fathering available, it could be argued that here's another instance of 'make it up as fathers go along' with the best of intentions in mind. Equally, it's assumed that involved fathers are actually <u>also</u> doing intimate fathering, but this, of course, is a stretch of understanding. There are sure to be some involved fathers who are not also focused on building emotionally strong relationships with their children. On this point, Johansson and Klinth[3] say the development of men's caring attitude towards their family members does not necessarily equate with them being more gender-equal, as there's a difference between being 'child-oriented' and enacting 'gender-equal parenting'. It's also important to mention that Dermott's research on intimate fathering was conducted with only British fathers as she wasn't investigating the extent to which her finding applies to other cultural groups.

Male emotionality is presumed to be in opposition to female identity, through emotional repression and self-estrangement, resulting in a gendered model of the 'emotional female' and the 'unemotional male'[4]. It has been argued that what has traditionally structured men's private lives is a type of 'limitive' emotionality, built on stoic principles. Jeroen Jansz[5] expands this emotionality discussion by considering that contemporary Western masculinity is focused on four characteristics: autonomy, aggressiveness, achievement and stoicism. Stoicism is described as "*control of pain, grief and vulnerable feelings*" and is the main attribute in creating a "*restrictive emotionality*" in men's daily performances of self. Indeed, bell hooks[6] builds on this by saying, "*Patriarchy demands of men that they become and remain emotional cripples*" – a stark message. This is surely why the time is ripe to consider men's emotions in their role as fathers and to capture more thoughtfulness on what stands in the way of intimate fathering, according to changing gender ideals.

In order to 'do masculinity', men have to borrow from available public versions of masculinity. And if emotions are to be understood as a set of practices[7] then there must be 'relational practices' employed to manage emotions. As an example, instead of immediately expressing a feeling, Jansz suggests that men usually resort to a logical and rational deduction. The very act of disclosing feelings is a risky endeavour since men might come across as vulnerable or weak in the process. By resisting or disguising this, men can maintain emotional distance in their close relationships, which helps them feel they have exerted control and preserved their autonomy. Being an intimate or engaged father is "*not only a social role but also an emotional identity*" with boundaries that are "*fluid, and in part, negotiated in relationships*"[5]. Alexandra Macht[8] shares more about men's diversion tactics, such as channelling them into an emotion that's in alignment with masculinity (anger, for instance) or concealing emotions. In doing this, men are able to maintain personas that are perceived as detached, cool and tough. This is one emotionality mechanism that reinforces 'dominance' and we can see this emotional control is a core element in the way status and power is constructed in the social world. But it's obvious the downside of such emotional strategies might be that it's hard for men to engage in meaningful and intimate relationships. Lacing up most feelings, other than ones that bolster a restrictive masculinity, is not a given in men's nature, but rather the result of a lack of practice.

I want to say something basic here that often gets left out of ordinary everyday comments about men and emotionality as well as in scholarly work on masculinity; men have within themselves a full range breadth of nuanced emotions all with the potential to fully express them. We know that men and women both experience emotions. It's not whether or not men *experience* the full gamut of emotions like women do – it's in how they display their emotions that we find the biggest differences. And it doesn't help that men are mocked for being emotionless robots (remember the survey respondent who mentioned being seen as a machine rather than as a human being?). Women and men experience emotions pretty similarly physiologically, however, women *show* much more emotion in most situations. And this would make sense since men feel pressure to abide by traditional male gender roles as they aren't permitted to display their emotions freely, as the female gender role encourages. So instead, they numb or stuff them. The gendered 'borders' of masculinity are depicted as "*impenetrable, representing absolute security, defence and control*", in contrast to feminine borders are perceived to be "*porous and flexible*"[9].

Fathers with SPUNK *feel* with new, emerging forms of masculinity. New forms of relating that disrupt old styles of numbing or stuffing emotions are important for men as fathers and for the children they're raising. The potential dysfunctional impacts of restrictive emotionality are far-reaching, with the effects of breaking free in some ways still unknown fully. Men are allowed to show a minuscule fraction of emotions – anger and apathy, in the main – with a common answer from boys and men being "*I don't know*" on enquiry about feelings (one of the best ways of detecting disconnection from their emotional source). Men, in the meantime, are ever cast as simple, ignorant creatures who have no feelings or emotional intelligence. But – *shock* – this is not true.

This is the point: when men abide closely to a restrictive male gender role, restrict their emotions, and focus on toughness and aggression, something negative begins to happen to their emotional development. The male psyche does not then know how to handle emotions at all – his own or anyone else's. So, the man becomes emotionally stunted, angry, and apathetic. This is the man who shuts down when his partner expresses anything (hurt, anger or frustration). It's the man who doesn't know how to deal with something sad or disappointing or wounding or embarrassing, so he turns to something like alcohol, sex, betting or silence. Or it's the man who gets angry when criticised or confronted because he doesn't know another way to handle feelings of shame. We all probably know this man or are this man. And we have the strict male gender role and our collective upholding of it to thank.

Shame researcher Brene Brown[10] discovered an interesting finding in her research on emotions. She learned we cannot selectively numb emotions. That is, when we choose to numb negative emotions like fear, sadness, shame or loneliness, we also simultaneously numb positive ones like gratitude, pride, excitement or happiness. Think about this for a moment.

Barrie Thorne's[11] work illuminates 'invisible social lines' that reproduce gender socialisation and differentiate boys from girls and vice versa in publicly shared spaces such as schools and homes. These invisible social lines include the inculcation of restrictive emotionality in boys, which lay down emotional foundations for men's lives, albeit cultural differences will obviously impact this.

As psychotherapist Nic Tovey[12] puts this: "*Possibly the most prominent and powerful realisation that I gained from my own experience with mental and emotional disease was the fact that I, as a man, grew up grossly ill-equipped to adequately navigate the varying terrain of my internal emotional landscape. What was also clearly evident was how this deficiency in basic life skills, not only my own but in all men, has an enormously negative impact on, not only we men but on the whole of society; our partners, our children, our fellow men, the greater community and the earth herself.*"

Given this backcloth, boys grow up in a patriarchal society that (at some point) means their emotional selves must be betrayed. Moreover, patriarchy often forces mothers to be the agents of that betrayal. Whether it's by suddenly or gradually withdrawing tender care and comfort that boys have had up till then, because "*boys don't cry, and men do not shed tears*"[13], or boys discovering their mothers don't know 'what it's like to be male' and are therefore wrong, so the only way to effectively defend themselves from violence is with some measure of violence. In

Boys Will be Boys, Clementine Ford[14] writes about a Twitter micro essay that went viral. She outlines how at a face painting party, a four-year-old boy asked for a butterfly to be painted on his face, but his mother said no, insisting he got something 'for boys'. The mother then turned to the boy's dad and had him confirm he didn't want his son having, in his words, "*a big old gay butterfly on his face*". The emotional assassination of boys involves sheering them in two. A cutting away of their tender, soft, gentle selves starts early.

Human beings develop habitual ways of acting and responding emotionally in given situations throughout life, but these habits are themselves the sedimentation of past patterns of relationships and actions. Yet masculinity is not an insular and unidimensional identity or a mere role to fit into because it is a continuously practised gendered identity. It takes committed practise to master embedded habits, whether dysfunctional or functional.

Let's dig into the concept of **self-care,** which historically has <u>not</u> been applied to men hardly at all as if they don't need to care for themselves. Instead, it's an industry peddling products to (mostly) women featuring #IAmEnough type slogans. Although it's still primarily targeted at women, self-care has started to appeal to men too. As I write, male and unisex beauty brands are betting on a sociocultural shift in their favour, partly spurred on by the impact of lockdown. The notion of men being disinterested in grooming is outdated. It highlights the importance of cultural nuance: "*In South Korea, it's very accepted that men wear makeup and there are some very popular men's brands. In the UK and US, there's still a mainstream attitude of the so-called 'alpha' male.*"[15]

Lux Alptraum[16] suggests that self-care just needs to be renamed life hacking because self-care reeks of vulnerability, whereas life hacking is all about improvements and performance. Tim Ferris[17] style all the way.

We can't talk about the emotionality of fathers and the reductionist propensity of Father Stunter Culture around emotionality without at least touching on men's mental health. Around 30% of people who use mental health services in the UK are men[18] despite the fact around 75% of suicides are male[19]. Having already covered that men are less likely to seek help than women, it's noteworthy that 50% of women who took their own lives had previously seen a mental health professional, whereas only 29% of men had[20]. The lack of treatment of men's mental health issues is one of the critical issues within male psychology[21].

Male depression is yet to be widely accepted as a clinical diagnosis, which is ludicrous given amassing evidence it's a valid clinical phenomenon. It's possible male depression is not recorded accurately on depression questionnaires because 'acting out' symptoms are not asked about. It's also likely depression is misrecorded as criminality or substance abuse disorders. Recently, bespoke male depression scales (Gotland, The Male Symptoms Scale, The Male Depression Risk Scale) detect male depression with higher accuracy as they include reference to risk-taking, anger attacks, and distraction coping strategies (gaming, sex/pornography, etc).

Cultural differences can be seen when we consider African cultures that characterise men as 'unable' to be irrational or emotional in the face of challenges or overwhelming events[22]. Consistent with this belief is the idea that the African male or female does not get depressed[23] which is equivalent to the hypothesis that Africans do not experience mental health challenges. For instance, depression across Black cultures was considered a sign of emotional weakness, and those who exhibit helplessness, worthlessness, or hopelessness, which are core symptoms of depression, are considered cowards. Most Africans are likely not to report their mental health symptoms or seek professional help and are more likely to seek religious help when faced with mental health problems without guilt or self-blame.

In a recent review of 25 years' worth of research[24] it was found that men experience anxiety at rates up to almost five times higher than average during their partner's pregnancy and the first year of parenthood. It is also estimated that 10.4% of men experience a male version of Postnatal Depression (PND), but it often goes undetected, most commonly in first-time fathers. Which brings us to our next set of data from the SPUNK Survey:

- When asked, "*I have experienced depression due to fatherhood*", respondents rated themselves on a continuum from extremely disagree through a continuum to extremely agree.

While 50.7% disagreed that they'd experienced depression, 26.8% definitely agreed they had, with the remainder 22.5% in a neutral neither agree nor disagree rating. More than a quarter of respondents in this survey therefore had or are suffering depression due to their fatherhood role.

- When asked, "*Do you have any disability?*", 6.4% of respondents identified as having a disability.

Roughly 15% of the world's population has some

kind of disability (including mental health and neurological conditions), yet just a fraction of those people identify themselves as people with disabilities. This is because, as a label, it's mired in stigma that people avoid the label[25]. Hence, it's likely that more than 6.4% of respondents are disabled.

> When asked, "*Do any of your children have disabilities?*", 16.8% of respondents answered that one of their children did.

This is above the estimated 11.2% of the 2.6 billion children and adolescents worldwide who were thought to be disabled[26]. I am making an assumption this is owing to our (overdue) growing definition of 'disability' and respondents full inclusion of not only mental health but also neurological and neurodiverse conditions, of which many require additional care on different levels. Raising disabled children demands shifts in family processes in order to meet the needs of all family members. In a beautiful book on the emotional lives of fathers caring for children with disabilities, Aaron Jackson[27] tells how his children "*existentially increased my emotional range*".

Much like we can't discuss fathers' emotionality without talking about mental health, neither can we discuss it without talking about the gender of their children. The gender of children seems to matter in not only the way fathers relate emotionally but also the content of what's discussed. Fathers of boys are expected to teach sons what it means to be a man, whatever version that is, and girls are taught anything from being like a princess to being a kick-ass strong woman. The sexualisation of girls is an area that fathers have the opportunity to affect for the better. For instance, Michael Vaughn[28] questioned why sexism starts so early. He asked how come his baby girl is a daddy's princess, why her clothes are form-fitting and revealing so she can be displayed/objectified. In contrast, boys' clothes are made bigger, more comfortable and designed for them to move around in. And then there are the "*Sorry boys, Dad says no dating*" on his newborn 'girls' onesie. As Vaughn questioned, who is going to date his zero-month-old daughter?

As his daughter grows up, here's hoping he'll also reject the idea of 'dates' with his daughter in a pseudo girlfriend vibe that feels creepy and ill-advised. (In reverse, mothers having dates with sons is just as creepy; this isn't some veiled paedophilic jibe at men.) Vaughn and his public campaign is a prime example of his social consciousness and emotional intelligence questioning dominant narratives about gender roles. Raising cute little princesses and tough boys to protect them is the natural order of life for many men. Truth is, this embeds a toxic mindset that girls are vastly different from boys and vice versa. Are we to believe that left without external judgement, boys wouldn't like glitter and teddies? There are plenty of grown 'masculine' men who yearn for a cosy blanket day on a sofa with a cuppa rather than anything gung-ho, right?! Point is, fathers *can* disrupt the way gender biases are inflicted on children. This is the crux of why fathers with SPUNK must FEEL or here's what will continue for our sons: "*I think many of us who wander around western culture as grown-ups in male skin grew into childish and/or adolescent images of what we thought men were supposed to become...It's no wonder we find ourselves in relationships, communities, organisations, institutions – and entire nations – filled with man-children and/or man-adolescents dressing the part and pretending.*"[29]

But there's hope. According to Niobe Way's research[30], as boys develop into young men, they tend to lose "*emotional acuity and insight*", meaning after their mid-teen years, men are less encouraged by society to reflect on, understand, and articulate what they're feeling. **Absolutely.**

In fact, I'd say this assessment is way too late as

this loss of emotional acuity and insight is already well advanced by mid-teens. Anyhow, Way points out that if they maintain emotional acuity past their mid-teens, it's because "*someone with a significant role in their life as an adolescent encouraged them to process and talk openly about their emotions.*" **This need not be a mother**. Nurturing these capacities in their early years will lay down foundations for young boys to withstand later bouts of peer pressure. By mid-teens, it is *way too late* to start teaching our children about empathy and a range of emotions.

Turning our attention back to the SPUNK Survey, I framed several different questions in order to try to get the heart of the subject matter here, starting with ideas around stereotypes:

- When asked, "*Please indicate how much do you agree with: I call out stereotypes when I see them*", 67.7% of respondents agreed they call out stereotypes when they see them, 13.9% disagreed they call out stereotyping, and 18.4% were neutral. And 32.3% are not necessarily calling out stereotypes when they see them.
- When asked, "*Please indicate how much do you agree with: I avoid stereotypes in my children's media*", 43% agreed they avoid stereotypes in their children's media. A whopping 46.2%

answered neither agree nor disagree, but 10.8% disagreed they avoid stereotypes. Hence 57% are not affirmative about avoiding stereotypes in their children's media.

Children's media is a *broad* category; it includes print (books, magazines, newspapers), television, movies, video games, music, cell phones, various software, and the Internet. The influence of this in children's lives is vast.

- When asked, "*I encourage my children to have a positive outlook on body image*", Nearly 85% agreed that they do, with just over 15% responding in a neutral category. No respondent disagreed with this statement.
- When asked, "*I feel comfortable with the shape of my body and my face*", over 36% of respondents do not agree with this statement.

Like it or not, we pick up attitudes and behaviours from our parents, and while some of these behaviours are healthy and positive, others can be damaging. This ripple effect is especially pronounced when it comes to body image, and fathers' role in this is not to be underestimated. Research suggests that mothers play a significant role in the development of their daughters' body image, but a Mental Health Foundation study[31] in the UK shed light on men's relationship with their bodies. In a survey of 2,103 males, almost one in twenty men said they had deliberately hurt themselves as a result of body image issues. And nearly three in ten adult men felt anxious because of body image issues. The 'Dad Bod' phenomenon is only possible if you're fit, but not too fit; if you have some fat, but not too much. This category has been positioned as the fifth option left just off the edges of our "*Cut, Ripped, Jacked, or Swole*" continuum[32]. But who decides who is which isn't clear. Nor is the answer as to whether or not it should be hailed as progress that the male body is now being subjected to a gaze almost as hyper-critical as that which has plagued women for centuries. It seems there's evidence from the SPUNK Survey to suggest body image issues in men are becoming even more pronounced, which increases the risks of men's poor mental health and the ripple effect passed to children.

In the SPUNK Survey, I asked an array of questions on fathers' confidence in providing sexual education as well as encouraging conversation around these topics (including listening to children's views). Reviewing responses, it's obvious there's still a way to go before men are confident in taking on the teaching/guiding role on the topic. Respondents were asked to select the rating that best described how confident they felt in each situation:

- When asked, "*How confident do you feel that you have adequate knowledge to provide sexuality education to your children?*", 7.4% said they are unconfident, 20.6% chose neutral, and 72% feel confident.
- When asked, "*How comfortable are you in talking to your child about sexuality?*", 13.2% said they are unconfident, 16.2% chose neutral, and 70.6% feel confident.
- When asked, "*How confident you are to encourage your child to ask questions about sexuality?*", 7.4% said they are unconfident, 29.4% chose neutral, and 63.2% feel confident.
- When asked, "*How confident you are to start up a conversation about sexuality with your child?*", 17.7% said they are unconfident, 26.4% chose neutral, and 55.9% feel confident.
- When asked, "*How confident you are to encourage your child to share their thoughts and feelings about sexuality?*", 7.3% said they are unconfident, 26.5% chose neutral, and 66.2% feel confident.
- When asked, "*How confident you are in listening to your child's views on sexuality*", 5.9%

said they are unconfident, 19.1% chose neutral, and 75% feel confident.

Apparent in these findings is that although some fathers are anticipating and guiding sexual education conversations with their children, others are unsure and insecure in this. Overall, there's a mismatch between just over half of fathers from this survey reporting confidence starting up a conversation about sexuality with their child and 75% of them feeling confident in listening to their child's views on sexuality. These findings have an implication for fathers seeking a less watchful focus while listening well. Fathers cannot leave these fatherly conversations to chance or assume that someone else in their child's life will feel more inclined to teach them.

Fathers with SPUNK need to be **leading** conversations on sex, body positivity and gender roles. Indeed, a missing area (from the SPUNK Survey) that must be included in (White fathers) conversations with children is the role of race in society.

And let's not forget that conversations around sex and sexuality open the doorway for parental bonding and the conversations about the more significant emotional, intimate and – yes – joyful conversations that fathers need to get in on; not only those around things like consent, protection and sexual health, but those around planning first dates, being a good partner, falling in love, handling heartbreak, and all the shades in-between.

The role of teacher and outward-facing-to-the-world-role model has been covered here already because fathers are vital to their children's lives[33]. This vital link begins with attachment formed with both parents based on nurture, but fathers have an added element of encouragement for their children to explore the world beyond the family. As Machin[34] says: "*This is why dads seem to have a disproportionate role in those elements of their child's development linked to operating in our social world including their language development and prosocial skills; sharing, caring, helping.*"

Fathers with SPUNK must teach their children sharing, caring and helping from emotionally regulated foundations within themselves. As Douglass[35] said, "*It's easier to build strong children than repair broken men.*"

Fathers with SPUNK aren't afraid to FEEL

I've already discussed this, but it needs to be hammered home and then some; an awful lot gets spoken about masculinity's privileges, particularly White masculinity, particularly White humans who identify as men. We know those privileges well.

But the more we narrow the range of activities

and stereotyped possibilities – the emotionality – of what it is to be a boy, and therefore a man, the more we narrow their range of emotional experiences and right to expressiveness.

Men get thrust into channels of life that aren't necessarily helpful for them and aren't helpful for anyone else either. The humanity that we disregard for males is a travesty. We need to reinfuse our understanding of what it means to be male with *human-being-ness.* Fathers with SPUNK embrace their emotionality in the face of strict stereotypes because they know, ultimately, this is the only way to shape a better future for their children (especially those that identify as male). Here are a few recommendations on how to achieve this:

- **CHALLENGE and CHANGE the toxic male emotionality PRISON:** There's one prison that holds more men captive than all the industrialised prisons in the world. This cellblock is customised for each inmate, with undetectable walls and a solid 'mental door' that locks from the inside – keeping the hearts of men isolated from society at large. It's called **Emotional Incarceration**[36]. For our boys to grow up to become empowered, emotional men (and fathers), we **HAVE** to challenge and change this prison and the erosion of emotional acuity and intuition.

- **TEACH boys to self SOOTHE:** I can't tell you the amount of content that exists around supporting toddlers with their emotional regulation – a vital and life-saving skill. But as mentioned, at a far too early age, the scale for boys begins to tip into the negative. Instead of recognising, acknowledging, processing, expressing, and understanding their emotions, they're encouraged to shut *everything* all down. We need to pinpoint the point at which this tipping happens and promote greater balance.
- **ALLOW men to be FULLY expressed human beings:** Boys DO cry – from sadness, anger, joy, happiness, grief, confusion, rejection – all of it. Men need to be able to be fully expressed human beings. Our collective discomfort at expressed male emotion is a, for lack of a better word, grotesque aspect of Father Stunter Culture and toxic masculinity. Instead of focusing on the gender of the individual as they process and express their emotionality, we need to focus on the human being.

One final note: take a stand on going on 'dates' with your kids. It's creepy.

FATHERS WITH SPUNK STICK

"I didn't see my first-born son for eleven years. His mum made it really, as in really, difficult for me, '*if you don't marry me, you're never going to see your boy*'. Contact centres, family court, back and forth, I'd drive a 400 mile round trip for an hour visit, to be told when I arrived '*he was poorly*'. This happened numerous times. I went to court, and it all went my way, winning both parental responsibility and a contact order.

None of it was ever enforced. That same 400 mile round trip with some spurious reason as to why I couldn't see him, yet no one thought to contact me to tell me ahead of the journey. It was now becoming a *game* I never wanted to play, nor a game I could ever win. When he was two, I made a decision, and I had to live by that decision – that I wasn't going to be in his life for the foreseeable future, it was too costly a price for me mentally, and whichever way I stepped I was gonna stand on a mine.

At the time, it was the right decision to make.

Looking back, it was still the right decision to make. '*Dad, are you there?*' was the message that came through on my Facebook messenger. He was thirteen, he had finally found me and made contact, and since then we've been steadily building a relationship. It's of course never going to be the same as it would have been had I been allowed to be in his life consistently, but we've got a nice, sensible, growing relationship now, sadly little shared history from those first years.

My own biological father wasn't really around when I was growing up, but I have my stepdad, who is, essentially, my dad. Interestingly when I was younger, I got into and won a fight at school. When I told my stepdad about it when I got home, he said, '*that's not something to be proud of*'. I know, if I had told my biological dad the same thing, his response would have been, '*well done, son, did you give him plenty?*' And that's the crucial difference – that fork in the road. Had I grown up with my biological dad, I think I would have grown up to be a pretty bad operator.

I think there's a bigger conversation to be had, around parental law and the reasons why fathers who would have stayed in their kids' lives, feel they can't. Children need their mothers, fathers, parents. It shouldn't be as complicated as some parents choose to make it."

BRAD BURTON, Motivational Speaker

"One of the issues that comes up time and time again is parental alienation, where one parent is alienating the kids against the other parent. I see the two sides of the equation through the work that I do, where there are dads who want to have that relationship with their kids, and in some, not all instances, they're prevented from doing so. I don't like dealing in absolutes, I know it's not all women that prevent dads from seeing their children, and I know there will be dads who just walk out and decide never to see their children again. But the reality is – most loving, caring mums want dads to see their kids, and most loving, caring dads want to carry on seeing their kids."

JOE HORTON, Founder of Guild of Dads

"It was a real jolt to me when my first son was born. The first nine months, while you're expecting and waiting for the baby, everyone's rallying around and wanting to know what you're having and if you've picked out a name. Then all of a sudden, when the baby's born, everyone disappears, and you're just left to get on with it. You're dealt this huge piece of reality; sleepless nights, being tired all the time. And if I am brutally honest, I couldn't handle it. I wasn't ready for this huge commitment, and drinking became my escape. When I went home, I wasn't ready to share the commitment, and that's where it started to go wrong. When I lived on my own again, the selfish part of me came out, I didn't have to handle this responsibility anymore. It was an easy way of life to slip into, and no one questioned me on it."

DAVID WILSON, Grey Area Drinking Coach

"I get asked to speak at different men's groups, and I don't do a lot of them because it's usually around issues of separation. I've found these groups are so filled with negativity and disrespect, I've realised I just can't be part of it. I would speak with these groups and tell them one of the utmost foundational aspects of being a good father is treating the mother with respect, and many of them just can't do it. Parents need to focus on what's best for their child, and what's best for their child is having a meaningful and respectful relationship with each other. Children are masters of body language, tone of voice – a lot of their communication is non-verbal. Children know what's going on between the parents and how both parents treat them. Fathers often don't see their role in this because there's so little weight on their shoulders, so little responsibility, if they get it wrong."

MICHAEL RAY, Solo Dad, Speaker & Author of *Who Knew?*

If there's one topic that polarises, no matter *who with* and *where* it's absent fathers. Fatherlessness is positioned as a public health crisis and, "*if it were classified as a disease, fatherlessness would be an epidemic worthy of attention as a national emergency*"[1]. An enormous body of work has been devoted to a lack of father presence and the absence of father involvement in children's lives. Extensive coverage describes the vast fallouts for children raised in father-absent homes, including:

- Poverty
- Reduced sense of physical and emotional security
- Behavioural and social problems
- Poor academic performance
- High crime
- Substance abuse problems
- Mental health disorders

From sexual behaviour, background demographics of prison inmates to mortality rates, pretty well everything is ~~blamed~~ explained by father-absent homes. It's fair to say the revolution over the last half-century in family structure has been *mostly* welcome; more accepting attitudes towards divorce and more autonomy for women has increased human freedom, and we know that variations beyond the traditional nuclear family can and do work. But a preponderance of the problems of fatherless families and the prevalence of 'family breakdown' has increased. Albeit, let's not peddle ideas about the collapse of heteronormative family structure as the root of all evils, as others seem more than capable of doing that.

As (many) women fought to be unshackled from the confines of their identity tied to reproduction and housework, so (some) men argue it's equally time to unshackle them in a raft of ways, not least away from work as a representation of their primary identity. Before we move further, let's not ignore men's position within the gender order legitimated by capitalism. Men must have access to economic resources to fulfil their patriarchal potential. Moreover, men are expected to guard-dog protect the institution of patriarchy to safeguard their positions of power within society. But this is not straightforward since the concept itself and forms of hegemonic masculinity become mobile, provisional and, if you like, ongoing projects, offering the potential for non-normative and egalitarian masculinities.

It's worth considering how misleading assumptions behind fatherhood research consistently position father involvement as **absolutely essential** or children are doomed to failure, whether that's poverty, prison or premature death. A challenge to the notion every child requires a father to successfully develop is possible, though hardly ever offered. Researchers Sear and Mace[2] asked whether children with absent fathers are likelier to die. They reviewed data on child survival from forty-three studies of populations around the world, mostly those without access to modern medical care. They found that in a third of the studies looking at fathers, children were more likely to survive childhood when their dad was around. But in the other two-thirds, fatherless kids did just as well. By contrast, every study of children without mothers found they were less likely to survive. "*That is not what you would expect to see if fathers are really vital for children to thrive,*" Sear says. Rather, she suspects what's vital are the jobs fathers perform. When a father is missing, others in the family or community can fill in: "*It may be that the fathering role is important, but it's substitutable by other social group members.*"

This could explain why there are numerous examples of people who succeeded without being raised with a father. Barack Obama became President of the

United States. Michael Phelps became the most decorated Olympic athlete in history. Both were raised primarily without a father. Although, Obama must surely be an outlier. In a 2008 Father's Day speech[3], he declared fathers are critical to the foundation of every family. Without fathers, children are destined to be unable to form secure bonds, lack self-esteem, are accident-prone, wheeze asthmatically, and become fat. The outlook is bleak or so we're led to believe, even while research on fatherhood still suffers from Western bias and US-centrism[4]. The majority of our fatherhood theory is built on thousands of studies on US fathers as if they are the norm, including data from the SPUNK Survey in which just over half of respondents reside in the US. Attention to single-parent families has focused on adverse outcomes for children of majority mother-headed families rather than, as Khadijah Martin[5] said, "*not fatherless…how about motherful?*". It's rare to find media coverage, for instance, where there's anything but disdain and hand wringing about inevitable outcomes for children raised by single mothers. But it isn't this that scorches conversation anytime fatherless families are raised. Mention absent fathers; prepare to duck for cover. Here's what came out of the SPUNK Survey on the topic:

- When asked, "*Are you a non-resident father for any of your children?*", Only 7.4% responded that they were a non-resident father to their children.

However, because of other responses, it became apparent the way this question was asked was problematic. Using this language suggests a child's main residence is elsewhere, with the unspoken assumption this is with the mother. This short-sighted question design shows how endemic this fixed view is. One respondent wrote to me on this, "*I am not a non-resident father. I have my daughter 50% of the time. Your survey did not allow for that option*". Point taken.

What this makes it impossible to say, with certainty, is the residency status of fathers and children in this survey; 7.4% is a low figure. When cross-matched with other information, it's likely *at least* half of a truer figure of approximately 18–20%. Non-resident parents emerge from the breakdown of a cohabiting relationship; some fathers have never lived in the same household as their children. As such, this survey included men who may never have been a resident father to their children and fathers who live with some biological and/or stepchildren but have non-resident children living in another household as well. Data on non-resident parents are not systematically collected typically and it's hard to recognise non-resident fathers in large surveys. It's also been suggested some fathers may not acknowledge they've non-resident children in surveys to avoid being identified by child maintenance services[6].

For much of the twentieth century, limited research showed it was common for non-resident fathers to lose contact with their children. Estimates from the early 1990s suggested that up to 74% of non-resident fathers lost contact with their children, with unemployed or low-income fathers most likely to lose contact[7]. There's a deep-rooted assumption that fathers who live apart from their children and are not in a relationship with the mother (who is usually the primary carer) are 'absent' and 'feckless', e.g., they are uninterested in their children and do not wish to provide financially for them[8]. But by 2016, 87% of fathers maintained contact with non-resident children; 38% several times a week, 21% in touch once a week, 28% in touch less than weekly but at least a few times a year, and 13% having no contact[9]. It's unclear what 'being in touch' means as this could be anything from a one-minute call to overnight or longer stays.

Ethnic background is a factor in the likelihood of being a non-resident father. In the UK, 14.7% (2.9 million) of families were lone-parent families[10];

63% of Black Caribbean children were growing up in lone-parent families, as were 62% of children in the 'Black Other' ethnic group. High instances of lone parenthood were also experienced by mixed ethnicity Black children. Black African communities have a lower rate of single parenthood at 43%, with South Asian and Chinese ethnic groups much lower than other groups, and the Indian ethnic group the lowest at just 6%. Indeed, Kopano Ratele[11] laments that constructs about Black men centre around notions of them being "*fundamentally damaged and damage-doing*" and, more specifically, indifferent and violently abusive. Black fathers are presented as "*frequently absent, unknown and undisclosed*" and are especially demonised as inherently problematic.

But conflating single-parent homes with the absence of father involvement gives a false picture because Black and White fathers are similarly maintaining contact with their children[12]. It's inaccurate to suggest that Black fathers' non-residency is evidence of their wholesale absenteeism from their children's lives since this just isn't true. It's also not been a stretch for many to assume associations between ethnicity and family breakdown and subsequent child welfare concerns, which presents a highly stigmatising narrative potentially placing a large number of (non-White) families under a position of scrutiny.

This focus on absenteeism means that much literature on contemporary fathering stems from a problem-solving rationale, ignoring the considerable number of fathers who maintain contact with children, thus framing non-resident fathers and their families as a problem that needs to be solved.

But let's move from problematic definitions and framing of non-resident fathers and instead view non-residency as a model of fatherhood amongst many others, rather than as a negative or a prohibitive position compared to co-residency. This approach recognises that, more broadly, fathering, parenting, and family relationships encompass a range of complexities. Just as not all resident fathers are the same, nor are all non-resident fathers.

I've already argued that contemporary fatherhood is centred upon personal connections between father and child(ren), often neglecting much of the mundane practicalities of parenting. This consequently results in a disparity between culture and conduct wherein men continue to do less care than mothers whilst expressing an intense commitment to, and connection with, their children. And since co-resident fathers can already feel treated as an adjunct in terms of parental status, it's not hard to imagine that non-resident fathers find services and interventions systematically exclude them as these operate on a one-family household model. One example of this is census data which only allows for children to be registered as living in *one household*, so figures on non-resident fathers can make it seem as if father-child relationships are non-existent, or at least not close. Researchers Goldman and Burgess[13] argue this is problematic because non-resident fathers often spend a great deal of time (up to and equal with mothers) with their children, but the role and positive outcomes associated with non-resident father involvement are often overlooked. The non-resident father's position is eroded.

As fathers adopt more intimate and involved roles, debates about 'good' fathering increase, with the actions and responsibilities of fathers also becoming increasingly 'moral'. Eyes to the SPUNK Survey once more:

When asked, "*In your opinion, has being a non-resident father changed your parenthood?*", qualitative responses in the open text boxes included:

- "*There is a distance now between us.*"
- "*Made me focus on not living in a toxic environment.*"
- "*Lack of contact has changed my ability to be the father I want.*"

- "*My children and I are closer than ever.*"
- "*It takes me at least a day with my son to turn around his negative thinking.*"
- "*I parent the way I feel is best for each child rather than deferring to their mother.*"
- "*I can't know my kids as well as when I lived with them.*"
- "*Grateful for the life we're building together, just us.*"

Outcomes from non-residency are complex, nuanced and not one bit inevitable, hence these variable response rates. It's well known that when asked to give feedback, humans tend toward an asymmetry in how we process negative and positive occurrences to understand our world, so that, "*negative events elicit more rapid and more prominent responses than non-negative events*"[14].

During the School for Fathers podcast interviews, I've listened to men talking about their lives and heard their thoughts on fatherhood generally, including other men as fathers. I've heard the phrase "*real men don't run away*" a number of times, sometimes off-air. This seems to strike at the heart of absentee father discussions. Fatherless families is a theme that ripples under the surface of conversation, occasionally emerging. This relates to guest's upbringing, commentary on fatherhood generally, and lived experience. Since I've interviewed hundreds of fathers, I've heard men asking the same questions over and over. These include the following, which I've loosely themed below.

Two caveats: it's impossible and unhelpful for me to provide *answers* for these enquiries, but my comments are injected here. The questions are conversation starters to hand to you, reader, for you to decipher where you stand on any given theme. Many of these questions could also be considered in terms of LGBTQIA+ fathers, but I'm conscious there's a myriad of nuanced questioning around fathers who emerge into their sexual identity after becoming fathers in the 'traditional' sense (with a heterosexual mother) and what this means in terms of absenteeism, residential status and contact.

The 'Fatherless Cycle':

- Do fatherless men create fatherless families?
- If having grown up fatherless and doing well in life, how can men answer *why my kids need me* and *what for?*
- How to co-parent with women with 'daddy issues' from being fatherless?

Fathers with no contact with their children:

- How can fathers (who say they love their children) abandon them?
- Why do loving fathers stop seeing or being in contact with their children?
- Fathers with sporadic contact with their children:
- Why do some fathers opt-in and opt-out of being a father whenever they want?

Fathers with no contact with their children and new families:

- How can and why do some fathers set aside/ leave their first family then rebuild new ones without a back glance?
- Why do some men become serial family builders, one family after the next then the next?

Contact with damaging fathers:

- Isn't it better for a 'bad father' to keep away/be kept from his children?
- Should self-aware damaging fathers, who choose to stay away, be supported with this decision?
- Who gets to decide what constitutes 'damaging'?

Fathers and financial provision:

- Why do fathers need to financially provide for their children when mothers are working?
- Why do some fathers turn their back on their children financially?

Fathers and the 'Package Deal':

- Are children a 'package deal' with their mothers?
- How come stepfathers become father-figures then move on from stepchildren if the relationship with their mother ends?
- Why do fathers not see stepchildren they've helped raise because they're no longer with the mother?

Parental alienation and contact disagreement:

- What happens when fathers are forced out and alienated by the mother of their children?
- Why do women dislike acknowledging that SOME women are the reason some fathers are kept from their children?
- What do you do when children want more contact with a father, but he doesn't want it?
- What do you do when children don't want contact with a father, but the father does want it?

Plenty of research shows that fatherless children who become fathers themselves are presented with both challenges and opportunities. In studies of fatherless fathers raising children, some men express difficulty understanding what they're meant to be doing as a father as they struggle to understand the role and become ambivalent, unsure and disconnected. Meanwhile, there are also fathers who've successfully thrived without fathers themselves and question the need for them in their children's lives. Growing up without a father does not have to bring negative consequences – it really does need repeating because the cacophony saying otherwise drowns out this possibility. One of the reasons boys grow into functional fathers (despite being fatherless themselves) is that many draw on memories of loving men who were influential in their own childhoods. From grandfathers, uncles, adult brothers, teachers, and best friend's fathers, boys draw on the fatherly examples available to them. Observing their friends interacting with their fathers, watching positive fatherly role models in the media and drawing upon their mother's parenting serves to skill them up with "*a set of behaviours far beyond biological reproduction*"[15].

As Annie McManus[16] writes to her small son, "*Your father stuck around, but a lot of fathers don't.*

And when they don't, it is with the assumption that the children will be the mother's consequence to manage". Children are somebody's consequence; most men try to do a better job than previous generations. Some find themselves incapacitated by their own parenting history, or reject the example they were given, which increases their motivation to be involved, whether co-resident or not.

"*They say girls with daddy issues are really good in bed,*" says Beck in YOU, the Netflix thriller series, encapsulating the narrative sexualising the relationship between fathers and daughters. There are countless sexual novels based on the psychological dynamic attributed to fatherless girls. For instance, fatherless women 'adopt' men as fathers[17]. It is said a father instils not only his beliefs in his children but also forms part of shaping his daughter's femininity – a big part of her identity. More notably, this influence (or lack of) is reflected in the daughter's romantic relationships. Daddy issues are suggested when abandoned daughters seek out an older man who will protect her or when she appears to lack the skills or judgment to make successful relationships. This description strikes me as describing a substantial percentage of women socialised to look for 'traditional' protective qualities in a mate. Fortunately, the idea that those of any gender can have daddy issues is becoming more widely accepted today. This is partially driven by pop cultures, such as the television show *Lucifer*, which acknowledges that men's adult behaviour can be impacted by their poor early relationships with their fathers, just as women can.

In a post on Emma Johnson's website[18], *Wealthy Single Mommy*, she explains when people consider why fathers leave children, they surmise one of two things. Either, 1). Men are irresponsible douchebags who abandon their children to mothers, who are left to raise the children with few resources. Or, 2). Women are conniving, malicious, entitled nut-jobs who alienate fathers from their children while taking all said fathers' money – all of which is supported by the family court system. Stark perspectives. And such bullshit.

The nuanced picture of why men don't have contact with their children is multivarious. To start with, three main constraining variables are literally at the tip: economic and social resources, family situation/re-partnering, and location. Logically, fathers in more disadvantaged positions have less contact with their children, which can be attributed to the expenses of maintaining and facilitating contact[19]. Other family commitments, such as resident children or new partners/spouses, can reduce fathers' financial, emotional, and time resources for their non-resident children; having a partner, particularly having additional children, reduces the likelihood of contact further. But housing and location also play a significant part in any contact. One study[19] of divorced fathers found they felt it best to leave the family home to cause as little disruption to children as possible. Moving from the family home and gaining suitable housing is considered an integral part of 'good' fatherhood. Unsurprisingly, when fathers live further away from their children, they're less likely to have regular contact. Moreover, the number of bedrooms in non-resident fathers' homes also influences contact with children, with fathers in less secure financial situations less likely to have contact with their children at all. Non-resident fatherhood can be associated with lower living standards. However, there are serious problems in drawing this conclusion as there's very little empirical research undertaken on 'family breakdown' affecting a father's financial situation. Additionally, some fathers gradually drift apart from their children. One of the strongest associations with contact is that the longer fathers and children live together, the more opportunities they have to develop close emotional bonds. This principle applies to cohabiting as well as married parents. Consistent with this assumption, it's been found fathers exhibited less-frequent contact when separations occurred relatively early in children's lives. The age of children also has a significant influence, with contact levels decreasing as children grow older[20]. Literature on non-resident fathers tends to define a gradual decline in contact as the typical trajectory. It's also worth noting paternal contact is not always a choice because some fathers may be sent to prison or deployed overseas if they're in the military.

Research[21] shows fathers tend to stay in contact more with sons than daughters – a trend that grows stronger as children get older. Is it that fathers share more interests with sons than daughters, or fathers feel an obligation to be a role model for their sons, or that mothers encourage fathers to interact more with sons than daughters? What is clear is that if the mother of the child or children remarries or cohabits with a male partner, some fathers step back from contact as if their position has now been usurped or is no longer needed. What is this baton handing over of fatherly responsibility about?

Thinking back to a topic I touched on in chapter one; you'll recall some respondents had difficulty determining who they consider they are father to and for. Looking at the data from the SPUNK Survey:

- When asked, "*How many children have you*

> *been a father figure for?*", 6.1% of respondents answered 'none.' When filtering our results by men who were non-resident parents (the child lives with the other parent, at least some or all of the time), this number increased to 16.7%.

This data seems to show that fathers who live with their children identify as father figures more than those who do not. Fathers who live away from their children describe themselves as feeling *less* like fathers, regardless of the age of the children. When comparing this question to "*How many children under 18 do you live with more than 50% of the time?*", the 'none' response didn't change more than 1%. This has implications for understanding the mindset around why, when, and how long fathers stick around once they become non-resident. It's as if proximity deepens the internal father identity; isn't this what men wrote to me about when asking "*how many children am I father to?*". This also seems obvious when we consider men's primary (legitimised) identity as one of 'worker' whereas, for women, society places a priority on the 'caring mother' identity. As mentioned in the introduction and limitations of this survey, this cannot be generalised to all men (a little more on that coming up) but it is noteworthy. What are the double-edged impacts of this, for men, children, and within society?

One of the most erroneous judgements about paternal contact relates to racial variations arising from differences in attitudes, values, and social mores that affect how fathers relate to children and co-parent with mothers. White fathers subscribe to a 'package deal' that typically links partner and paternal responsibilities. Relationship dissolution makes continuing contact with children of this package deal fragile at best, nonexistent in most instances.

For some fathers, this means when a relationship ends, the link between himself and the children is weakened, and he may not continue contact *since the primary link between himself and the woman is broken*; the woman **and** the children are **THE package deal**. Black fathers do not share this package deal approach and instead collaborate more readily with the mothers of their children. In contrast, fractured relationships with White father's ex-partners more often stands in the way of involvement and contact[22]. Although father involvement and contact after a non-marital birth declines steeply for all race and ethnic groups, Black fathers experience the <u>least</u> drastic decline compared to White and Hispanic fathers[22]. Even in the case of incarceration, which diminishes involvement overall[23], minority fathers maintain contact with their children more often than White fathers[24]. It seems although Black fathers are especially positioned as errant, it may be fruitful to explore further the ways White fathers construct and reconstruct ongoing paternal responsibilities on relationship breakdown. White fathers are not necessarily (most) in contact with or involved with their children.

Emma Johnson[25] argues that a move towards equal parenting time would support financial equality between men and women. In a parenting world where it's presumed shared parenting is the norm, no financial payment from one parent to the other would be needed, she argues.

In Kentucky, US, for instance, a shared parenting bill was passed a few years ago on the grounds that shared parenting is presumed in the best interest of the child. There are exceptions made to shared parenting if there's a history of domestic violence, and other factors are still considered, such as the child's proximity to their school. But Johnson suggests, "*Even if you earned less than your partner, begin to think about ways to earn more money in the years post-divorce and how to become less reliant on child support if you currently receive it.*" She rallies women on by saying, "*Think big. The system is set up for you, as a woman, to be financially dependent on your [ex-husband]. You are better than that. And not to mention, compliance with child support is very low.*"

She cites the average collection rate for child support from non-custodial parents as around 65% nationwide in the US as of 2018. On the one hand, ditch support from your ex on the grounds you can earn this yourself, but realistically, you're probably not going to get the money from your ex anyway, so you might as well forge ahead without him. And for those who *do* pay, from Johnson's perspective, it's shared parenting all the way. I like this a whole lot. Especially in that utopian world where a gender pay gap is just a nasty dream. Johnson hops and skips Pollyanna style over pay disparities and, of course, suggests her strategy will equalise money between genders/parents. Then again, she does have a blog post about selling your wedding ring for money – maybe this income will pay the winter heating bill?! But she's right to point to non-payment of maintenance as an area of reform.

Here's what respondents from the SPUNK Survey had to say on the topic:

- When asked, "*Approximately what percentage of your income do you pay in financial maintenance for your child/children?*", respondents answered from none through to percentage ratings of less than 10%, 11–30%, 31–50%, and more than 50%.

This question was NOT reserved for non-resident fathers. Instead, my interest in fathers' assessment of their overall financial input was across all fathers. The median was 11–30% of income paid towards their child/children. Significantly, just over 20% stated they pay nothing. Whether this was because the word 'maintenance' was used (which can denote alimony in the UK) or whether these fathers are not financially contributing is not obvious. At the other end of the scale, more than 10% pay more than 50% of their income. These findings demand further investigation and I'm curious about how mothers might answer the very same question.

Whether installing shared parenting as standard with no maintenance (in which case men's work patterns, or the women they live with, will need to alter to accommodate increased parenting) **OR** legal mechanisms requiring fathers to be financially responsible for their children, this is an area that needs to be addressed. Too many children are exposed to poverty because their fathers don't stick around.

There are many reasons why fathers step away from contact with their children, including, of course, parental alienation. Drawing on the work of Dr Clawar and Dr Rivlin and their study[26] published by the American Bar Association, they say, "*Caution must be exercised in judging that the point of no return has been reached. We have seen numerous cases where children have been successfully deprogrammed by making radical changes*". But for some fathers, it is too late, and children have been bad-mouthed, alienated, and brainwashed to an extent that, "*It means that you have exhausted all efforts to reclaim your children's love... Their alienation is too severe and entrenched. Your ex is unable or unwilling to stop the bashing and brainwashing. Your attempts to get the court to intervene effectively have met with failure.*"[27]

The strong cultural narrative of good fatherhood as being present – in the sense of being physically near one's children and involved in the care of them – gives way to a possibility to re-envision good fatherhood by also including an alternative narrative in which leaving children may not be such a bad thing. Some (possibly lots of) fathers, contrary to the narrative of callously ditching children, are instead choosing to step away as a form of protection *for the children* and themselves. In this narrative, men describe stopping fighting for their children as a defeat but that it could, in the end, turn the children into stable, resilient individuals untainted from the toxicity of any battle between the parents. Fathers work through this moral dilemma and (for some) emotional torture and find their way through everyday life, often with an accompanying backcloth of grief and recovery. In the Resources section, you'll find supporting information to assist you if you're in a situation that includes parental alienation.

Meanwhile, on the idea of 'bad' fathers, it's important to note fathers' neglect, abuse, domestic violence, and coercive control of any kind are directly associated with childrens diminished psychological wellbeing in adulthood. Professionals and systems (e.g., family courts) often aim to maintain relationships between children and domestically violent fathers, "*overrid[ing] children's and mothers' right to protection*' and '*compromis[ing] their safety*"[28]. Children who have post-separation contact with fathers who are perpetrators in these contexts can experience acute fear, distress and physical ill-health, and are sometimes subjected to physical, emotional and/or sexual abuse during contact visits. There's been a move internationally towards criminalising controlling and coercive behaviour in family and intimate relationships[29]. But so far, these focus on situations with adult perpetrators and adult victims. There's a need for these laws to acknowledge that coercive control can also be perpetrated by a parent against a child under sixteen years old. Children's experiences as victims and survivors of coercive control must gain greater recognition and support.

There are fathers who <u>do not stick around</u> actively

being their children's father, depending on how you define 'being a father'. Some offer financial support but have no contact with their children; others have no contact and no financial input. There are more permutations. None of this necessarily means men don't view themselves as fathers. This identity (can) and does live on whether the material circumstances change or not. There are men who are not involved in any parental alienation situation, who are not economically disadvantaged, who have the inner and external resources to be involved in the raising of their children, but who choose to make what I've been told are 'clean breaks'. Some men who talk with me about this say it's about starting again and not having to deal with the failure of their relationship and, by association, the fallout from this with the children. Others talk about momentum lost in the first six months of relationship breakdown that affect father-child relationships to the extent men feel they can't regain a place in children's lives. Others talk of regret at walking away and years of rationalising why this might be best/better for their children. In the case where a stepfather enters the family, some men realise they suddenly/slowly relinquish their role as if they're no longer needed.

There are as many reasons for men not sticking as there are snowflakes. No situation is the same.

Fathers with SPUNK STICK Around

As we've covered, children undoubtedly benefit when they have strong father figures and role models around them but who those figures and role models can be is varied. As Sear[2], whom I mentioned at the start of this chapter, advises – fathering can be substituted by others within a community.

So, *is* it fair to say fathers with SPUNK stick around? Perhaps it is more accurate to say that fathers with SPUNK know *when* to stick around, what that means for them and the children they're sticking about for, and they're clear on *why* they're sticking around. They don't take the easy way out. Fathers with SPUNK know their role and purpose as fathers and everything that entails. They gather inner counsel on their place through also being a father who FEELS. Fathers who leave, it could be said, are often acting from a limited range of knee-jerk emotions that follow the dissolution of a relationship (anger, for example). With stronger emotional grounding comes acumen about the set of unique and nuanced circumstances, for how they stick around.

How, then, do men as fathers go about achieving this? There are no easy answers; remembering no situation is the same. A couple of starting points:

- **Establish the WHEN, WHY, HOW and EMOTION for sticking around (or not):** Walking away for fathers is (mostly and for many (White) men) impeccably easy. It's a rare instance when men are quizzed, judged, or condemned for having walked away from children, biological or otherwise. I am not for one moment suggesting this isn't a polarised situation; some fathers agonise, fight, and have to give up, and there are some who lean into 'walking away' as an assumption as if it's just the thing they do. Why? Because there's a mother who will stay. Men are the ones who tend to say, "*I don't want any drama*" and "*I don't want no grief*". Interesting turn of phrase that last one; it gives a clue to the source of not wanting to feel anything. I believe that an inability to deal with the emotions associated with leaving leads some fathers to *shut it all down*. Not sticking, walking away, alienation, low or no contact – whatever you want to call it – is the accompanying action associated with not being able to feel the enormity of emotions associated with fatherhood. As we've covered, fathers with SPUNK FEEL; they do not do what is often easiest for many men and bury deep the complexity of emotion that not only comes with being a father but also must accompany walking out on children they've previously cared for. Ownership and responsibility over choosing to leave and the knowledge that it is (sometimes) possible to return are essential here. Dig deep into your answers to these questions. Courage (and a full spectrum of emotional awareness) is required.

- **Broader systemic CHANGE and ACCOUNTABILITY is NEEDED:** A large part of the reason fathers can so readily walk away are the societal narratives and Father Stunter Culture that all say they're in the right to be able to do so. Mothers will still be there, right? Current societal structures that favour men also shore up Father Stunter Culture around fathers' ability to walk away. And it isn't just that men walk away with the result being they don't see their children; many walk away knowing that (somehow) someone is going to pay for their children to be fed and clothed. As cited, non-collection of maintenance in the UK is a pressing issue. While Child Maintenance Service (CMS) does have the power to enforce payments (including taking non-paying parents to court, removal of passports or driver licenses, and imprisonment) it is rare these are enforced[30]. According to Deighton Pierce Glynn Law[31], during COVID-19, "*CMS have been running a skeleton service, in which they are no longer chasing or enforcing non-payment and are allowing non-resident parents to reduce or withdraw payments on 'verbal evidence' alone. This has effectively provided an open door for non-resident parents to stop paying.*" This also goes back to notions of flexible working, workplace policies around paternity and parental leave, more prominent and robust shared parenting bills and policies – this is a levelling up of our collective consciousness about holding fathers accountable across the board. Apart from that, there's ongoing societal complicity where men and women don't challenge fathers who leave children. Men are much more likely to ask each other, "*what happened to your car? Why did you get rid of it?*" than "*what happened to your kids? What do you mean you've left them?*" And women, who on hearing a father say, "*I've got six kids, but I only see two of them*", default to replies of, "*Oh, poor you*", instead of calling into question HOW and WHY. You don't need to be a parent to care about this and change the script. We must stop avoiding the conversation simply because it makes us uncomfortable; someone needs to feel bloody uncomfortable here, and it cannot be our children.

FATHERS WITH SPUNK RISE: THE FUTURE

"Men need to step up and put as much effort into parenting as women have been doing. One of the ways we can do that is by bringing together more men – more fathers – to connect and communicate and encourage each other. It's not about berating, nagging or pushing men; it's about showing them another way to do things and letting them know that it's okay to step outside of just being the provider. I've seen first-hand the positive outcomes that come out of this…to see other dads doing things differently, having fun, being involved, building a community of men like them – and that's when parenting growth can happen"

NIGEL CLARKE, TV Presenter and
Founder of Dadvengers

"It's always been about and always will be about personal choices and personal responsibility. What I wanted to do was exactly what I wanted to do, when I wanted to do it, how I wanted to do it, and to whoever I wanted to do it too. There were certain choices available to me that I just did not align with. So I made other choices. That way of thinking and being points to me being in pain and not knowing it. It points to me being confused and not understanding. It points to me not being willing to ask for help or knowing how to ask for help, which is the other piece of the whole mentality I bought into about what it meant to be a man – this idea that I don't have to ask for help because – as a man – I already have all the answers. I can figure it out for myself. I can do it on my own, and if I can't figure it out, I can just bull my way through."

ELDRA JACKSON III, Co-Executive Director;
Inside Circle

"Overcoming the bad bits of masculinity and the default settings we've been raised with requires we take on, tackle and actively see how we can change. There's a lot of legroom, a lot of scope, and long road men need to go down to change the traditional view of masculinity and create a new one. I think fatherhood, in a very real way, is a huge part of that.... But, let's be honest, it's not something we can neatly package up – there's no one guide to this kind of thing. It's an individual journey, and what matters is that you're able to recognise it in yourself and begin to change it. That's how we begin to change the cultural narrative – and that's why it's been great to see more men starting to speak about this. In reality, fathers don't have the stories to show us what to do in the same way mothers do. The cultural depictions of fathers in contemporary media are quite shallow, stereotypical, and continuations of these uber-masculine men. We have to raise the question of self-awareness to be able to recognise that, along with self-confidence and the support of family, friends, culture and media to then act on it."

DAVID WILLANS, Founder of BeingDads

This is a time in our cultural history when we can create profound change. We can choose to seize this moment as an opportunity to learn something from the pandemic and make sure that our world is an equitable place to live and parent in. The many challenges to fathers and fathering within the Father Stunter Culture at this historical moment can be seen as both deeply entrenched, inhumane treatment of men and significant opportunity to create new conditions. We do not have to choose one or the other; it can be both. In acknowledging the emotional assassination of men (as one practice that's re-inflicted and repeated till men are split in two) new conditions can also emerge. Holding horror for the breadth of damage to, between and from men ought not to mean we abandon hope of more for them, and for our sons.

We could take heart from the mobilisation of what academics call 'The Manosphere', a loose amalgam made up of men angry with the state of gender politics. Men like Mike Buchanan[1], the British leader of the Justice for Men and Boys (And the Women Who Support Them) who spout that, "*Men are stripped out of their families and become walking wallets because that suits the state. It's a very well documented feminist objective of forty years to destroy the nuclear family.*" But taking heart from their *ability to assemble* around injustice is the point, not what they congregate around. Their hatred of feminist ideals and feminists are infamous but rally on they do. International Conferences on Men's Issues (ICMI's) are described as 'magical bubbles' where men get together in places where men aren't hated. "*It's amazing what happens when men get together and you don't chain them*", is how Paul Elam (men's rights activist) warbles. And as Buchanan, tells us, "*Women have enjoyed equality of opportunity in the west for over half a century and still they cannot compete with men. I recently made an important decision. I've decided it's time for everyone in the men's rights movement and beyond to stop pretending that women will ever compete successfully with men.*"

These men bring hope even though their targets are sections of society who identify as feminists. There's solace and celebration to be had in watching men rise – because it shows it's possible – albeit not in the direction these men insist on going. To march backwards or even onwards (from Buchanan's perspective) in which men's character and mental health are measured by their "*readiness to say no to women*" smacks of men fighting for their right to defend patriarchy. Plenty of men get involved in struggles for gender justice and seek to change harmful norms and practices of masculinity, simply because it's the right thing to do. Even when men cannot see personal benefits in gender equality, they still have a responsibility to promote greater equality.

Father Networks have been growing steadily across the world. The National At Home Dad Network began back in the early 1990s in the US and has been dedicated to providing advocacy, community, education, and support for families where fathers are the primary caregivers of their children. Their purpose continues to be empowering fathers and championing a culture that recognises them as capable and competent parents. In the UK, expansion of networks for fathers has grown steadily, though the focus of these is broader than for at-home dads. The Fatherhood Institute, DadsUnlimited, Fathers Network Scotland, Guild of Dads, DadsHouse, ThisDadCan, DadsRock, DadLaSoul, and Dadvengers are just a few of the UK father support networks and lobbying groups doing stellar work as part of the social change that needs to happen. Additionally, podcasts on and for fathers have established themselves as key ways men grow and support one another. The extent to which these are social change making machines differs; some are pure entertainment, others more hybrid in purpose and impact. Whether a network, podcast or both, each agrees we must be interested in men as fathers. And many provide safe space for fathers to be vulnerable with each other so they can work towards expanding the parochial boundary of what it means to be a 'good father'.

As long as any systematic inequalities persist, those with privilege have an ethical responsibility to do what we can to change the system, right?! In the case of men and fathers, this responsibility may be more obvious to those men who are working for social justice in their own lives, for example, for economic or racial justice. But men increasingly recognise their struggles are related to women's struggles for gender justice. Beliefs about domination and subordination that lie at the heart of gender inequality play a fundamental role in other forms of injustice by 'naturalising' relations of domination, for example, of rich over poor, of White over Black. When men demand a gender-just society, it is not for women alone; it is necessary for men themselves. Men <u>must mobilise</u> to work for themselves and women and all other sexual minorities, and they need to take leadership to work beside other men in taking a public stand. They <u>must</u> walk the walk, as well as talk the talk. Our final look at the SPUNK Survey data provides some excellent insights on this.

When asked, "*Fast forward twenty years and fatherhood has changed for the better. What changes have happened to make this so?*", respondents had a lot to say. Here are some of their words:

- "*Better attitudes to fathering as a default.*"
- "*By definition, fatherhood is not a competition.*"
- "*Society recognises that men are as good at caregiving as women.*"
- "*Formal education about what it means to be a father.*"
- "*Men are enabled, encouraged and expected to be held equally responsible for raising the next generation.*"
- "*Men getting more paternity time off and that this is socially acceptable.*"
- "*Men knowing what to expect fatherhood will be like.*"
- "*Society sees the role of father as important as mothers.*"
- "*Equal role of father-mother nurturing body & mind.*"
- "*Paternity leave is the norm.*"
- "*Men's EQ has risen.*"
- "*Equal status with mothers in society's eyes. This will only happen if women are equal in society and work.*"

- *"Men are seen as carers."*
- *"The world wakes up, and men start to learn how to express themselves."*
- *"We are not passive bystanders."*
- *"People just don't see the dad as this other in the parental relationship. We can be caring and show our feelings. We don't always have to be the disciplinarian."*
- *"Better mental health and less stigma."*

Refashioned fatherhood twenty years ahead is father-centric, father-inclusive and father-friendly, at least from these father's hopes. They signal the direction they hope to go in. Not one father in this survey wants to uphold hegemonic masculinity or patriarchal practices in the style of Justice for Men and Boys, which reminds us that men have choices as to whether they accept patriarchy or work collectively against it. For men to rise in this way, a de-programming, releasing, and shedding of embedded habits will need to begin and ripple through our communities. As one respondent wrote, "*I swore to myself that I would do my bit in society by breaking my own habits to make it a better place for myself and for my child*". Obviously, such a seismic shift has to start early, with the values we instill in our children. The same respondent went on to say, "*I've committed to raising my son as gender neutral as I can, but it's going to take a lot more than me doing this to create a better world*". Mobilisation of men rising as activists for themselves, and others involves working to strengthen men's consciousness of their own ability to make change and their capacity to take action together with others[2].

But most men struggle to speak out against sexism and abuse, not because they're bad people, but because patriarchy impacts us all, and the pressure to conform to it is intense. There must be a willingness to take a critical perspective and recognise places where old gender patterns are reproduced. "*Men are often bad at recognising that because it doesn't serve them to recognise that*" and, "*It's hard when you go through life imagining yourself as the hero of the story to suddenly recognise yourself as the villain. We have read a thousand articles about the emotional labour that falls on women, but men need to work on this and say, 'where do we make gender assumptions and how do we change them?*'", says Jordan Shapiro in *Father Figure: How to Be a Feminist Dad*[3]. As men organise collectively, transforming their subjectivities and practices must be prioritised. This is why father networks are so important as they facilitate conversation and social actions that have the potential to regenerate and rescript fatherhood. Men must play their part in reconfiguring their modes of practice and ameliorating systemic inequalities. "*Men, I encourage you to challenge the status quo – to begin again and reach further – and break free from misconstrued masculinity so you can embrace your humanity*", battle cries author Jason Wilson[4]. Moreover, Shapiro argues[5], "*we can't do it as effectively as we might like until we're willing to reimagine fatherhood as less dominant, less paternalistic, and not necessarily masculine.*"

And in this, men and women must join together because handling this burden alone is impossible. Unbuilding the scaffolding of the structural barriers that make it hard for fathers to be highly involved will need allies and partners. And, although Helene Cixous said[6], "*It's up to you to break the old circuits*", I'd revise that to "*it's up to* **us** *to break the old circuits*".

One of the greatest obstacles to changing institutional culture, and in particular challenging patriarchal practices and attitudes within any given institution, is the sense that such practices and attitudes are too deeply entrenched to be changed. Hence, an important task confronting anyone working for change at the institutional level is to hold out a vision for how things could (and must) be different. The symbiotic relationship between the Mother Stopper and Father Stunter cultures cannot be transformed by changes for one gender without concern for the other. Real change must come at the level of attitudes, hearts and minds, as well as legislative reforms. The quote artist Michael James Schneider shared in a post on Instagam[7] comes to mind; "*Dividing and conquering is a White supremacist tactic. Uniting together is a radical act.*"

Bottomline; women must fight for men's rights whether men want them to or not.

In this context, it is important that male activists model the change they would like to see in the world by not taking over the struggle from women or seeking to 'protect' women from 'bad' men, but rather we have to change the conversation if we have any hope of creating a more equal future. If we change our expectations of ourselves as mothers, and men as fathers, to one of true equality, **we all win**.

A while ago I wrote and published a post on Facebook titled *Fuck Fathers Day*. I had all but forgotten about this until I came across it while looking for something else. My Facebook post was not based on blanket experiences I myself have had, but more from listening to the experiences of **so** many others; from my podcasts, my online community groups, and anecdotal confidences in both my personal and professional spheres. At the time of me writing it, Facebook was awash with mass celebration of good men and much loved, emotionally-present fathers

– in person and across social media. "*Grainy pictures of corduroy-wearing fathers in the 70s/80s cuddling dungaree-wearing children alongside shinier images of the current generation, embracing modern fatherhood*"[8] praised fathers for their sleeves-rolled-up, active, loving parenting. No one seemed to be voicing the obvious. (And YES, I *know* it's not *all* men and not *all* fathers – we've already established this retort only seems to crop up when we are finding fault with men and not women.) Here's what I wrote:

Fuck Fathers Day
I cannot stand by and watch the unbalanced story roll on by.
There are too many shits out there who let their kids down.
Fathers who were engaged, loving and present but POOFT they disappear into thin air.
Fathers who kept in touch then it all got a bit much so they gradually slid out the door.
Fathers who flat out say they're moving on. Then do it without a glance back.
Fathers who would rather stop work than pay maintenance.
Fathers who don't call, don't seem to care and don't remember they have kids with little hearts.
Fathers that would rather make their exes life worse

than focus on their children's welfare.
Fathers who become fathers to other children and then (eventually) repeat the insane pattern of leaving, again.
Fathers who 'help out' as their real-life is their career.
Fathers who think fatherhood is only about the fun stuff; cue sports, bike rides, handyman skills.
Fathers who think being Uncle Daddy is enough.
Fathers who choose themselves over and over.
Fathers who emotionally hurt their kids over and again.
Fathers who treat some kids as best and others as second best.
Fuck Fathers Day.
What Fathers have I forgotten? Shout them out.
(And yes there ARE wonderful fathers, those aren't the ones I mean.)

Unsurprisingly, as a result of speaking out, this post garnered cheers from *men and women alike.*

The heart of this book is that a significant change is long overdue in how we think about fathers, fatherhood, fathering and parenting overall. There are times in my past where I've contributed towards the Father Stunter Culture and I am building out my consciousness on this so I can stand against it. If I want to see the changes I know, from speaking to *literally* hundreds of fathers and mothers (and the standing ovation they gave my Facebook post), we all want to see in the ways we view, speak to, for and about parenting, we must RISE up independently and together to make it happen; we must hold each other accountable like never before.

The only way fathers will do that (with women as allies and partners) is to be fully invested in understanding the problems that need to be solved. If we don't want to be banging on about the lack of equality in society, on repeat, for decades to come (I'm tired of it, aren't you?), we all have to get that we are equally responsible for and part of the solution. Moving on from the responsibility-reluctance, Uju Asika calls[9] that, "*whole not-all-men-do-this push-back*", is a place where men as fathers ~~can~~ must get interested enough to hold themselves accountable for how they, "*behave within the system…relate to other men, [and] hold them to account*".

Launching the narrative and practices of fatherhood into an inclusive future where it belongs requires fathers to be empowered, enabled and enforced to take on this fresh kind of **SPUNK** they'll need to DO, SHARE, CARE, FEEL and STICK for themselves, and for their children.

I hand it to you, reader, to determine how **YOU** will **RISE** to make this radical act happen.

ACKNOWLEDGEMENTS

This has taken a village and I'm deeply grateful to the wonderful team who have encouraged, supported and assisted me in making this book possible.

Warm thanks go especially to School for Fathers Podcast guests who have shared their stories and lives with so many. Thank you to each and all. Thank you to those guests who gave generous permission to be featured and quoted in this book: Joe Horton, Rob Gorski, Jamie Beaglehole, Ian Dinwiddy, Nigel Clarke, Ying Tan, Michael Ray, Chris Lambert-Gorwyn, Dan Knowlton, Dan Flanagan, David Willans, Tim Taylor, Ken Mossman, Brad Burton, David Wilson, and Eldra Jackson III.

I'm also grateful to behind the scenes whizz Marie Cruz, without whose diligent podcast editing skills the show would never be the big success it is. Kudos to you for all you do.

I'm truly thankful for those who completed the SPUNK Survey and those who spread this across the world. I'm honoured you trusted me with your experiences and stories. Thank You. Gratitude must go to the awesome survey team, with an extra special mention to Lisa Barclay for her acumen, cheerleading and wisdom.

School for Mothers Podcast guests have been working in the background to make sure this book sees daylight, and I can't say a big enough thank you to everyone. It's in all our best interests to work together, and I appreciate your solidarity as we pick up the opportunity of a more (gender) equal and just society.

Huge acknowledgement must go to the Triumph Press team; thank you for the opportunity. And to Chief Editor Elaine Mead, linchpin and gold standard in editing.

It's a golden ticket to be wrapped by Rodrigo Corral and his team genius. There's little wonder your book covers are world known. Thank you.

Sincerest thanks to Alexandra Broomer, a brilliant mind, for the kindness, guidance, and unwavering support that has seen me through this journey.

To my family. Somehow despite you, I got this written – special love to those who were epic and dealt with the brunt of my fervour for this work. You know who you are.

To Dickie, my steadfast companion with a heart of pure love, thank you.

To my father, Zbigniew Malina, for always coaxing me on and for teaching me persistence. Disowning me for this book title, what can I say? I'd understand.

RESOURCES

This book forms part of a bigger conversation I've been bringing together across different online and offline communities. These communities are filled with empowered and vital voices from women, men *and* children, on how we create the types of father- (and parent)-hood the world needs.

The conversation doesn't stop with this book – it **must** keep going. An excellent place to start are the individual chapter reference sections. I've also included a selection of valuable resources below.

Podcasts Hosted by Danusia Malina-Derben:

- **School for Fathers Podcast** – School for Fathers explores modern working fatherhood with brilliant fathers. They mull over and find solutions for the challenges fathers face as they reposition their roles in work, the family, and society. Expect vulnerable conversation and insights that blow fresh air into what we know about men as working fathers. Find episodes on all pod streaming services and www.schoolforfathers.com.

- **School for Mothers Podcast** – Created to stretch traditional narratives around working motherhood and bring ambitious, talented, and diverse, often underrepresented female voices to the forefront of conversation. School for Mothers podcast episodes upend outdated perspectives by interrupting the noise surrounding women about how they should 'be' once they become mothers. Find the podcast on all pod streaming services and www.schoolformothers.com/podcast.

Dismantling Toxic Masculinity

- **The Mask You Live In (Film)** – *The Mask You Live In* follows boys and young men as they struggle to stay true to themselves while negotiating America's narrow definition of masculinity: https://therepproject.org/the-mask-you-live-in-watch-from-home/
- ***Deep Secrets* by Niobe Way (Book)** – *Deep Secrets* reveals how we tell ourselves a false story about boys, friendships, and human nature. Way argues boys are experiencing a "crisis of connection" because they live in a culture where human needs and capacities are

given a sex (female) and a sexuality (gay) and discouraged for those who are neither.

- ***Mascupathy: Understanding and Healing the Malaise of American Manhood* by Charlie Ronaldson & Randy Flood (Book)** – Revolutionising thinking about men, this book deals with the notion that most men's conduct is capricious or malevolent. Instead, they conclude it's a product of a socialised disorder, "mascupathy" – a pathology of masculinity – that describes an exaggeration of masculine traits and a reduction of feminine characteristics.

Father Communities

- **Guild of Dads Podcast**- Featuring weekly interviews with visionary men who have taken action towards creating the life they want, Guild of Dads also speaks to top experts about relationships, self-care, health and fitness, social contribution and finances: https://www.guildofdads.com/
- **The Autism Dad** – The Autism Dad details the ups and downs, joys and challenges of being a single father to three Autistic children. In the podcast of the same name, guests talk about the topics and issues relevant to us all:

https://www.theautismdad.com/

- **Daughter-Father Dance Podcast** – A daughter-father conversation demonstrating how love wins despite our differences – and, sometimes, because of them: https://www.daughterfatherdance.com/
- **Inspiring Dads** – Inspiring Dads aims to help stressed dads balance work and fatherhood, and build meaningful connections with their partners and children: https://www.inspiringdads.co.uk/
- **Dadvengers** – Whether you're a father, a mother, a soon to be dad, a grandad, a grandma, a carer, or parenting professional – Dadvengers is a community supporting dads on their journey through parenthood. With blog posts, a podcast, live dad chats, meetups and dad walks there are so many ways to engage with this forward-thinking fatherhood organisation: https://dadvengers.com
- **Dad La Soul** – Dad La Soul is a revolutionary grassroots movement that challenges the status quo and provides men with opportunities for social inclusion. Made by dads, for dads: https://www.dadlasoul.com/
- **The Fatherhood Institute** – The Fatherhood Institute's vision is a society that gives all

children a strong and positive relationship with their father and any father-figures: http://www.fatherhoodinstitute.org/

- **DadsUnlimited** – DadsUnlimited supports the well-being of dads through family breakdown by mentoring them, helping them to achieve a positive ongoing relationship with their children and improving co-parenting relationships: https://www.dadsunltd.org.uk/
- **Fathers Network Scotland** – Promoting the physical, mental and emotional health and wellbeing of fathers in Scotland through the provision of support to men in all aspects of their role as fathers: https://www.fathersnetwork.org.uk/
- **ThisDadCan** – ThisDadCan's vision is that every man has the chance to succeed at parenting and to resource men to be empowered, positive role models: https://www.thisdadcan.co.uk/about/
- **Dads Rock** – Dads Rocks aims to improve outcomes for children in Scotland to ensure the best start in life by providing support to Dads and families: https://www.dadsrock.org.uk/

Gender Diverse Perspectives

- **Outspoken Voices Podcast** – Outspoken Voices is by and for LGBTQ+ parents, people with LGBTQ+ parents, grandparents and everyone else who is part of these family journeys: https://www.familyequality.org/outspoken-voices-podcast/
- **Transgender School Podcast** – An honest mother-daughter conversation that's different from most: https://transgenderschool.org/podcast/
- **Daddy & Dad Blog** – The Daddy & Dad blog is dedicated to the highs and lows of adoptive parenting and seeks to respond to the latest LGBT news and current affairs: https://www.daddyanddad.co.uk/
- ***Raising Them: Our Adventure in Gender Creative Parenting* by Kyl Myers (Book)** – In this illuminating memoir, Kyl delivers a liberating portrait of a family's choice to dismantle the long-accepted and often harmful social construct of what it means to be assigned gender from birth.
- ***Stuck in the Middle with You: A Memoir of Parenting in Three Genders* by Jennifer Finney Boylan (Book)** – A father for six years, a mother for ten, and for a time in

between, neither, or both, Boylan has seen parenthood from both sides of the gender divide.

Parental Alienation

- **Absent Father Podcast** – This podcast is all about the impacts of growing up with an absent or distant father. Hear from guests as they share what they have learned and the impacts of growing up fatherless: https://absentfatherpodcast.com/
- ***Divorce Poison: How to Protect Your Family from Badmouthing and Brainwashing* by Richard Warshak (Book)** – *Divorce Poison* offers a blueprint for effective response. Learn how to distinguish different types of criticism, how and why parents manipulate their children, how to detect these manoeuvers, and how these practices damage children.
- **DadsHouse** – DadsHouse's long term aim is to tackle the causes of parental alienation through research, raising awareness and legal reform. They believe it's about the child's right to be cared for and raised by both parents equally: https://www.dadshouse.org.uk/

REFERENCES

INTRODUCTION & A NOTE ON SPUNK

1. Malina-Derben, D (2021). *NOISE: A Manifesto Modernising Motherhood.* London, Triumph Press.
2. Leonard, P., & Malina, D. (1994). Caught Between Two Worlds: Mothers as Academics, in S. Davies, C. Lubelska, and J. Quinn (Eds.), *Changing the Subject, Women in Higher Education* (pp. 29–41). London: Routledge.
3. SPUNK etymology. Retrieved from: https://www.etymonline.com/word/spunk
4. Murphy, M. L. (2011, August 18). *Spunk and Spunky.* Separated By a Common Language. https://separatedbyacommonlanguage.blogspot.com/2011/08/spunk-and-spunky.html
5. Sepinwall, A. (2021, December 9). *'And Just Like That...' is Missing the Funk and the Spunk.* Rolling Stone. *https://www.rollingstone.com/tv/tv-reviews/and-just-like-that-review-1269034/*
6. Somers, K. (2021, May 22). *What's on the other*

side of hard for the Suns? Armpits and underwear, for starters. The Arizona Republic.

7. https://eu.azcentral.com/story/sports/nba/suns/2021/05/22/suns-get-experience-hard-first-round-matchup-lakers/5208850001/
8. Debruge, P. (2021, October 10). *'The Tender Bar' Review: A Better-Than-Ever Ben Affleck Plays the Uncle Any 9-Year-Old Wants'*. Variety. https://variety.com/2021/film/reviews/the-tender-bar-review-ben-affleck-1235085686/
9. Kimmel, M. (2012). *Manhood in America: A Cultural History* (3rd ed.). New York: Oxford University Press.
10. Scourfield, J. (2005). Suicidal Masculinities. *Sociological Research Online*. 10(2), 1–15.
11. Greenfieldboyce, N. (2016, May 25). *For Female Fruit Flies, Mr. Right Has The Biggest Sperm*. NPR. https://www.npr.org/sections/health-shots/2016/05/25/479183334/for-female-fruit-flies-mr-right-has-the-biggest-sperm?t=1639494447305
12. Poppick, L. (2017, June 7). *The Long, Winding Tale of Sperm Science…and why it's finally headed in the right direction*. Smithsonian Magazine. https://www.smithsonianmag.com/science-nature/scientists-finally-unravel-mysteries-sperm-180963578/

13. Monty Python (1983). *The Meaning of Life.* United International Pictures, British Board of Film Classification.

FATHER STUNTER CULTURE & THE RESEARCH BEHIND THIS BOOK

1. Malina-Derben, D. (2021). *NOISE: A Manifesto Modernising Motherhood.* London: Triumph Press.
2. Creswell, J., & Poth, C. (2017). *Qualitative Inquiry and Research Design: Choosing among Five Approaches.* London: SAGE Publications Ltd.
3. Andrews, A., & Squire C. (2013). *Doing Narrative Research* (2nd ed.). London: SAGE Publications Ltd.
4. Young, S. R, & Massey S. G. (2021). *LGBTQ+ Studies: An Open Textbook.* Lumen Learning: Open Textbook. https://courses.lumenlearning.com/suny-lgbtq-studies
5. Kilkey, M. (Ed.). (2007). *Disabled Fathers: Identifying a Research Agenda.* Fatherhood Institute: Working Papers in Social Sciences and Policy No 20.
6. Redshaw, M., & Henderson, J. (2013). Fathers' engagement in pregnancy and childbirth:

evidence from a national survey. *BMC Pregnancy and Childbirth*. 70(13).

7. Bornstein, M. H., Putnick, D. L., Lansford, J. E., Pastorelli, C., Skinner, A. T., Sorbring, E., Tapanya, S., Uribe Tirado, L. M., Zelli A., Peña Alampay, L., Al-Hassan S. M., Bacchini, D., Bombi, A. S., Chang, L., Deater-Deckard, K., Di Giunta, L., Dodge, K. A., Malone, P. S., & Oburu, P. (2015). Mother and Father socially desirable responding in nine countries: Two kinds of agreement and relations to parenting self-reports. *International Journal of Psychology.* 50(3), 174–185.
8. Easterby-Smith, M., & Malina, D. (1999). Cross-Cultural Collaborative Research: Toward Reflexivity. *Academy of Management Journal.* 42(1), 76–86.
9. Solnit, R. (2012, August 20). *Men still explain things to me*. The Nation. http://www.thenation.com/article/169456/men-still-explain-things-me
10. Harrington, C. (2020). *What is Toxic Masculinity and Why Does it Matter?* Men and Masculinities. London: SAGE Publications Ltd.
11. Merriam Webster Online Dictionary (2021). Word of the Year 2017. https://

www.merriam-webster.com/words-at-play/woty2017-top-looked-up-words-feminism

12. Shapiro, J. (2021, February 3). *We Need More Feminist Dads.* Nautilus, https://nautil.us/issue/95/escape/i-want-to-be-a-feminist-dad
13. Dollahite, D. C., Marks L. D., & Olsonm. M. M. (2002). Fathering, Faith, and Family Therapy. *Journal of Family Psychotherapy.* 13(3–4), 259–289.
14. Vincent, N. (2006). *My Year Disguised as a Man*. London: Atlantic Books.
15. Mossman, K. (2021, March 21). *Terminal Adolescence.* Cirrus Leadership Blog. https://www.cirrusleadership.com/blog/gwtxtm8j1ceohzz263xr7drc95v5wj
16. Heilman, B., Barker, G., & Harrison, A. (2017). *The Man Box: A Study on Being a Young Man in the US, UK and Mexico*. Washington, DC and London: Promundo-US and Unilever.
17. Morin, A. (2020, November 25). *What is Toxic Masculinity*? VeryWell Mind. https://www.verywellmind.com/what-is-toxic-masculinity-5075107
18. Ngozi Adiche, C. (2014). *We Should All Be Feminists.* New York: Anchor Books.
19. Webb, R. (2017). *How Not to Be a Boy*. London: Canongate Books.

20. Kimmel, M., & Wade, L. (2018). Ask a Feminist: Michael Kimmel and Lisa Wade Discuss Toxic Masculinity. *Journal of Women in Culture and Society.* 44(1).
21. Ferguson, H., & F. Hogan. (2004). *Strengthening Families through Fathers: Developing Policy and Practice in Relation to Vulnerable Fathers and their Families.* Centre for Social and Family Research, Department of Applied Arts, Waterford Institute of Technology for the Department of Social and Family Affairs. http://www.welfare.ie/en/Pages/Families-Research-programme.aspx
22. Poole, G. (2015, November 9). *Is Machismo the Cause of the Male Suicide?* The Telegraph. http://www.telegraph.co.uk/men/thinking-man/is-machismo-the-cause-of-the-male-suicide-emergency/
23. Hooks, b. (2004). *The Will to Change: Men, Masculinity, and Love.* New York: Washington Square.
24. Whitehead, S. (2002). Men and Masculinities: Key Themes and New Directions. *Contemporary Sociology.* 32(5).
25. Cambridge Dictionary (2021). *Father, Fatherhood, Fathering.* London: Cambridge

University Press. https://dictionary.cambridge.org/dictionary/english/father#dataset_cald4

26. Oxford Language Dictionary (2021). *Mother, Motherhood, Mothering*. Oxford: Oxford University Press. https://languages.oup.com/dictionaries/
27. Daoud, E. (2021, February 16). *ANU gender researchers suggest changing terms 'mother', 'father' to be more gender-inclusive*. 7News Australia. https://7news.com.au/lifestyle/anu-researchers-suggest-changing-terms-mother-father-to-be-more-gender-inclusive-c-2174442
28. O'Reilly A. (2014). *Mothers, Mothering and Motherhood Across Cultural Differences*. Canada: Demeter Press.
29. Johnson, M. S., & Young, A. A., Jr. (2016). Diversity and Meaning in the Study of Black Fatherhood. *Du Bois Review: Social Science Research on Race*. 13(01), 5–23.
30. Obama, B. (2021, May 13). *Barack Obama Redefines What It Means to Be A Man*. Art of Power Podcast: WBEZ Chicago.

FATHERS WITH SPUNK DO

1. Maguire-Jack, K., Gromoske A. N., & M. Berger L. M. (2012). Spanking and Child

Development during the First Five Years of Life. *Child Development.* 83(6), 1960–77.

2. Shapiro, J. (2021, February 3). *We Need More Feminist Dads.* Nautilus. https://nautil.us/issue/95/escape/i-want-to-be-a-feminist-dad
3. Preston, E. (2021, July 8). *Most Male Mammals Have Little to Do With Their Kids. Why Are Humans Different?* The Wire. https://science.thewire.in/the-sciences/most-male-mammals-have-little-to-do-with-their-kids-why-are-humans-different/
4. Machin, A. (2019). *The Marvel of the Human Dad.* Aeon. https://aeon.co/essays/the-devotion-of-the-human-dad-separates-us-from-other-apes
5. Milanich, N. B. (2019). *Paternity: The Elusive Quest for the Father.* Cambridge: Harvard University Press.
6. Sayer, L. C., Bianchi S. M., & Robinson, J. P. (2004). Are Parents Investing Less in Children? Trends in Mothers' and Fathers' Time with Children. *American Journal of Sociology.* 110(1), 1–43.
7. Marsiglio, W., Day, R. D., & Lamb, M. E. (2000). Exploring Fatherhood Diversity: Implications for Conceptualizing Fatherhood Involvement. *Marriage & Family Review.* 9(4).

8. Lamb, M. E., Pleck, J. H., Charnov, E. L., & Levine, J. A. (1987). A biosocial perspective on paternal behaviour and involvement. In J. B. Lanaster, J. Altmann, A. S. Rossi, & L. R. Sherrod (Eds.), *Parenting across the Lifespan: Biosocial perspectives* (pp. 111–142). New York: Hawthorne.
9. Henz, U. (2019). Fathers' involvement with their children in the United Kingdom: Recent trends and class differences. *Demographic Research*. 40(30), 865–896.
10. GQ Magazine (2018, October 31). State of Man Report. https://www.gq-magazine.co.uk/article/gq-state-of-man
11. Alcoff, L. (2006). *Visible Identities: Race, Gender and the Self.* Oxford: Oxford University Press.
12. Cumming, E. (2021, October 29). *I'm terrified it might be my last chance': the rise of the pre-baby stag do.* The Guardian: Family Section. https://www.theguardian.com/lifeandstyle/2021/oct/29/im-terrified-it-might-be-my-last-chance-the-rise-of-the-pre-baby-stag-do
13. Wahl, J. (1949). *A Short History of Existentialism*. New York: Philosophical Library.
14. Montigny, F., & Lacharité, C. (2005). Perceived parental efficacy: Concept analysis. *Journal of Advanced Nursing*. 49(4), 387–96.

15. Fatherhood Institute (2021, November 19). *Dads Shut Out: fathers and maternity services during the pandemic.* http://www.fatherhoodinstitute.org/2021/dads-shut-out-fathers-and-maternity-services-during-the-pandemic/

FATHERS WITH SPUNK SHARE

1. Hochschild, A., & Machung, A. (2012). *The Second Shift: Working Families and the Revolution at Home*. New York: Penguin Books.
2. Malina-Derben, D. (2021). *NOISE: A Manifesto Modernising Motherhood.* London: Triumph Press.
3. Goodsell, T. L., & Meldrum, J. T. (2010). Nurturing fathers: a qualitative examination of child–father attachment. *Early Child Development and Care.* 180(1–2), 249–262.
4. Habib, C., & Lancaster, S. (2010). Changes in identity and paternal-foetal attachment across a first pregnancy. *Journal of Reproductive and Infant Psychology.* 28(2), 128–142.
5. Fathers Network Scotland (2021). *Lockdown II Dads Survey*. https://d3n8a8pro7vhmx.cloudfront.net/fathersnetwork/pages/4666/attachments/

original/1616803358/210323_FNS_lockdown_2_Survey_2021_Findings_Report.docx_%282%29.pdf?1616803358

6. GQ Magazine (2018, October 31). State of Man Report. https://www.gq-magazine.co.uk/article/gq-state-of-man
7. Oakley, A. (1984). *Taking It Like a Woman.* United States: Random House.
8. Powell, D. (2019). *Appropriated Ambition; A Narrative.* In F. Arnold & S. Brody (Eds.), *Psychoanalytic Perspectives on Women and Their Experience of Desire, Ambition and Leadership.* United Kingdom: Taylor & Francis Ltd.
9. Bianchi, S. M., Milkie, M. A., Sayer, L. C., & Robinson. J. P. (2000). Is Anyone Doing the Housework? U.S. Trends and Gender Differentials in Domestic Labor. *Social Forces.* 79(1), 191–228.
10. Lyonette, C., & Crompton, R. (2015). Sharing the Load? Partners' Relative Earnings and the Division of Domestic Labour. *Work, Employment and Society.* 29(1), 23–40.
11. American Family Survey (2021). *Resilience in the Face of Challenges American Families in the Second Year of the Pandemic.* https://www.aei.org/wp-content/uploads/2021/09/AFS-Report-2021.pdf?x91208

12. West, C., & Zimmerman, C. D. (1987). Doing Gender. *Gender and Society.* 1(2), 125–51.
13. Van der Lippe, T., Treas, J., & Norbutas, L. (2017). Unemployment and the Division of Housework in Europe. *Work, Employment and Society.* 1(20).
14. Wajcman, J. (2015). *Pressed for Time.* London: University of Chicago Press.
15. Ruppanner, L., Branden, M., & Turenen, J. (2017). Does Unequal Housework Lead to Divorce? Evidence from Sweden. *Sociology.* 1(20).
16. Norman, H. (2017). Paternal Involvement in Childcare: How Can it Be Classified and What Are the Key Influences? *Families, Relationships and Societies.* 6(1), 89–10.
17. Waltzer, S. (1998). *Thinking About the Baby: Gender and Transitions into Parenthood.* Philadelphia: Temple University Press.
18. Coltrane, S. (2000). Research on Household Labor: Modelling and Measuring the Social Embeddedness of Routine Family Work. *Journal of Marriage and Family.* 62, 1208–33.
19. Cadbury Heroes Survey (2019, October 7). Referenced in, *Over half of parents would love their family to spend more time together.* SWNS Digital. https://swnsdigital.com/uk/2019/10/

over-half-of-parents-would-love-their-family-to-spend-more-time-together/

20. Norman, H., Elliot, M. J., & Fagan, C. (2018). Does Fathers' Involvement in Childcare and Housework Affect Couples' Relationship Stability? *Social Science Quarterly*. 99(5).

FATHERS WITH SPUNK CARE

1. Khazan, O. (2016, October 24). *Emasculated Men Refuse to Do Chores – Except Cooking*. The Atlantic. https://www.theatlantic.com/health/archive/2016/10/the-only-chore-men-will-do-is-cook/505067/
2. Ruxton, S., & Burrell, S. R. (2020). *Masculinities and COVID-19: Making the Connections.* Washington: Promundo-US.
3. Hood, J. C. (1986). The Provider Role: Its Meaning and Measurement. *Journal of Marriage and the Family.* 48(2), 349–359.
4. Shirani, F., Henrood, K., & Coltart, C. (2012). Why Aren't You at Work? Negotiating Economic Models of Fathering Identity. *Fathering: A Journal of Theory, Research, and Practice About Men as Fathers.* 10(3), 274–290.
5. Diduck, A., & O'Donovan, K. (Eds). (2006). *Feminist Perspectives on Family Law.* London: Routledge-Cavendish.

6. Strategy& (2019, March). *Women in Work 2021: The Impact of Covid-19 on Women in Work.* PWC Report. https://www.pwc.co.uk/economic-services/WIWI/women-in-work-2021-executive-summary.pdf
7. Blanchot, M. (1949). In G. L. Bruns (1984). *Language and Power.* Chicago Review. 34(2), 27–34.
8. LaRossa, R. (1988). Fatherhood and Social Change. *Family Relations.* 37(4), 451–57.
9. Kangas, E., Lamsa, A. M., & Heikkinen, S. (2017). Father Managers (Un)Doing Traditional Masculinity. In A. Pilinska (Ed.), *Fatherhood in Contemporary Discourse: Focus on Father.* Newcastle: Cambridge Scholars.
10. Goodsell, T. L., & Meldrum, J. T. (2010). Nurturing Fathers: A Qualitative Examination of Child–Father Attachment. *Early Child Development and Care.* 180(1–2), 249–262.
11. Machin, A., (2019). *The Marvel of the Human Dad.* Aeon Online. https://aeon.co/essays/the-devotion-of-the-human-dad-separates-us-from-other-apes
12. Knight, C., & Brinton, M. (2017). One Egalitarianism or Several? Two Decades of Gender-Role Attitude Change in Europe. *American Journal of Sociology.* 122, 1485–1532.

13. Sanders, M., Zeng, J., Hellicar, M., & Fagg, K. (2016, February 3). *The Power of Flexibility: A Key Enabler to Boost Gender Parity and Employee Engagement.* Bain & Company. https://www.bain.com/publications/articles/the-power-of-flexibility.aspx
14. Koslowski, A., Blum, S., Dobrotić, I., Kaufman, G., & Moss, P. (2021, August). *17th International Review of Leave Policies and Related Research 2021.* Leave Network. www.leavenetwork.org/annual-review-reports/review-2021/
15. Petts, R. J., Knoester, C., & Li, Q. (2018). Paid Paternity Leave-Taking in the United States. *Community, Work & Family*. 23(2).
16. Topping, A., (2021, April 26). *Shared Parental Leave: Scrap 'Deeply Flawed' Policy.* The Guardian. https://www.theguardian.com/money/2021/apr/26/shared-parental-leave-scrap-deeply-flawed-policy-say-campaigners
17. Pragmatix Advisory Ltd (2021, November 12). *Flexonomics: The Economic and Fiscal Logic of Flexible Working.* Essex, UK. https://www.srm.com/media/3369/2021-11-12-confidential-flexonomics-a-report-by-pragmatix-advisory-for-sir-robert-mcalpine-and-mother-pukka.pdf
18. Clawson, D., & Gerstel, N. (2014). *Unequal*

time: Gender, Class, and Family in Employment Schedules. New York: Russell Sage Foundation.
19. Munsch, C. L., Ridgeway, C. L., & Williams, J. C. (2014). Pluralistic Ignorance and the Flexibility Bias: Understanding and Mitigating Flextime and Flexplace Bias at Work. *Work and Occupations.* 41(1), 40–62.
20. Rudman, L. A., & Mescher, K. (2013). Penalising Men who Request a Family Leave: Is Flexibility Stigma a Femininity Stigma? *Journal of Social Issues.* 69(2), 322–40.
21. Chung, H. (2019). Dualization and Subjective Employment Insecurity: Explaining the Subjective Employment Insecurity Divide Between Permanent and Temporary Workers Across 23 European Countries. *Economic and Industrial Democracy.* 40(3), 700–729.
22. Berdahl, J. L., Cooper, M., Livingston, R. W., & Williams, J. C. (2018). Work as Masculinity Contest. *Journal of Social Issues.* 74(3), 422–438.

FATHERS WITH SPUNK FEEL

1. Dermott, E. (2008). *Intimate Fatherhood: A Sociological Analysis.* London/New York: Routledge.
2. Baumann, Z. (2003). *Liquid Love: On the*

Frailty of Human Bonds. Cambridge: Polity Press.

3. Johansson, T., & Klinth R. (2008). Caring FathersThe Ideology of Gender Equality and Masculine Position. *Men and Masculinities*. 11(1), 42–62.
4. Lupton, D. (1998). *The Emotional Self: A Sociocultural Exploration*. London: SAGE Publications Ltd.
5. Jansz, J. (2000). Masculine Identity and Restrictive Emotionality. In A. H. Fischer (Ed.), *Gender and Emotion: Social Psychological Perspectives*. Cambridge: Cambridge University Press.
6. Hooks, b. (2004). *The Will to Change: Men, Masculinity, and Love*. New York, Washington Square.
7. Scheer, M. (2012). Are Emotions a Kind of Practice (and Is That What Makes Them Have a History)? A Bourdieuan Approach to Understanding Emotion. *History and Theory*. 51(2), 193–220.
8. Macht, A. (2020). *Fatherhood and Love: The Social Construction of Masculine Emotions*. Oxford: Palgrave Macmillan.
9. Skeggs, B., & Moran, L. J. (2004). Queer

as Folk: Producing the Real of Urban Space. *Urban Studies.* 41(9), 1839–1856.

10. Brown, B. (2021). *Atlas of the Heart: Mapping Meaningful Connection and the Language of Human Experience.* London: Vermillion.
11. Thorne, B. (1993). *Gender Play: Girls and Boys in School.* New Jersey: Rutgers University Press.
12. Tovey, N. (2015). *About Nic.* Nic Tovey. http://www.nictovey.com/about-nic/
13. Goodey, J. (1997). BOYS DON'T CRY: Masculinities, Fear of Crime and Fearlessness. *The British Journal of Criminology.* 37(3), 401–418.
14. Ford, C. (2020). *Boys Will Be Boys: Power, Patriarchy and Toxic Masculinity.* UK: Oneworld Publications.
15. Morosini, D. (2021, June 7) *How to prepare for a men's beauty boom.* Vogue Business. https://www.voguebusiness.com/beauty/how-to-prepare-for-a-mens-beauty-boom
16. Stiller, C. (2019). *Modern Manhood: Conversations About the Complicated World of Being a Good Man Today.* New York: Tiller Press.
17. Miller, T. (2012, November 20). *I'm Tim Ferris, and This Is How I Work.*

Lifehacker. https://lifehacker.com/im-tim-ferriss-and-this-is-how-i-work-5961603

18. Smith, K. L., Matheson, F. I., Moineddin, R., Dunn, J. R., Lu, H., Cairney, J., & Glazier, R. H. (2013). Gender Differences in Mental Health Service Utilisation Among Respondents Reporting Depression in a National Health Survey. *Health.* 5(10), 1561–71.
19. Affleck, W., Carmichael, V., & Whitley, R. (2018). Men's Mental Health: Social Determinants and Implications for Services. *The Canadian Journal of Psychiatry.* 63(9), 581–589.
20. Kung, H. C., Pearson, J. L., & Liu, X. (2003). Risk Factors for Male and Female Suicide Decedents Ages 15–64 in the United States: Results From the 1993 National Mortality Follow Back Survey. *Social Psychiatry and Psychiatric Epidemiology.* 38(5), 419–426.
21. Liddon, L., & Barry, J. (2021). *Perspectives in Male Psychology: An Introduction*. NJ: Wiley Blackwell.
22. Van Heerden, A., Msweli, S., & Van Rooyen, H. (2015). Men Don't Want Things to be Seen or Known About Them: A Mixed-methods Study to Locate Men in a Home-based Counselling and Testing Programme in

KwaZulu-Natal. *South Africa, Afr. J. AIDS Res.* 14(4), 353–359.

23. Alang, S. (2016). "Black Folk Don't Get No Severe Depression": Meanings and Expressions of Depression in a Predominantly Black Urban Neighborhood in Midwestern United States. *Social Science Medicine.* 157.
24. Lieferman, J. A., Farewell, C. V., Jewell, J., Lacy, R., Walls, J., Harnke, B., & Paulson, J. F. (2020). Anxiety Among Fathers During the Prenatal and Postpartum Period: A Meta-Analysis. *Journal of Psychosomatic Obstetrics & Gynecology.* 42(2).
25. Bogart, K. R., Rottenstein, A., Lund, E. M., & Bouchard, L. (2017). Who Self-Identifies as Disabled? An Examination of Impairment and Contextual Predictors. *Rehabilitation Psychology.* 62(4).
26. Olusanya, O. B. (2020). Global Burden of Childhood Epilepsy, Intellectual Disability, and Sensory Impairments. *Paediatrics.* 146(1).
27. Jackson, A. J. (2021). *Worlds of Care: The Emotional Lives of Fathers Caring for Children with Disabilities.* California: California University Press.
28. Vaughn, M. (2021, March 26). *Tell Me About the Moment You Realised Sexism is*

Real [Video]. TikTok. https://www.tiktok.com/foryou?is_from_webapp=v1&item_id=6943602323541216517#/@ericasaysstuff/video/

29. Mossman, K. (2021, March 24). *Terminal Adolescence.* Cirrus Leadership Blog. https://www.cirrusleadership.com/blog/gwtxtm8j1ce0hzz263xr7drc95v5wj
30. Way, N. (2013). *Deep Secrets: Boys' Friendships and the Crisis of Connection.* Cambridge: Harvard University Press.
31. Mental Health Foundation. (2019, May 13). *Body Image: How We Think and Feel About Our Bodies.* https://www.mentalhealth.org.uk/publications/body-image-report
32. Ellis, P. (2021, January 29). *What Does It Even Mean to Have a 'Dad Bod' Anymore?* Men's Health. https://www.menshealth.com/fitness/a35322745/what-is-dad-bod/
33. Machin, A. (2021, February 8). *Dads: The Untapped Mental Health Taskforce.* Anna Machin. https://annamachin.com/dads-the-untapped-mental-health-taskforce/
34. Machin, A. (2018, June 18). *International Fathers Mental Health Day.* Anna Machin. https://annamachin.com/international-fathers-mental-health-day-18th-june-2018/

35. Confehr, C. (2017, September 22). *Frederick Douglass Descendant Offering Education to Prevent Human Trafficking.* The Tennessee Tribune. https://tntribune.com/frederick-douglass-descendant-offering-education-prevent-human-trafficking/
36. Wilson, J. (2019). *Cry Like a Man: Fighting for Freedom from Emotional Incarceration.* Colorado: David C Cook Publishing.

FATHERS WITH SPUNK STICK

1. National Center for Fathering (2021). *The Extent of Fatherlessness.* Fathers Online. https://fathers.com/statistics-and-research/the-extent-of-fatherlessness/
2. Sear, R., & Mace, R. (2008). Who keeps children alive? A review of the effects of kin on child survival. *Evolution and Human Behavior.* 29(1), 1–18.
3. Obama, B. (2008). *Text of Obama's Fatherhood Speech.* Politico. https://www.politico.com/story/2008/06/text-of-obamas-fatherhood-speech-011094
4. Shwalb, D. W., Schwalb, B. J., & Lamb, M., E. (2013). *Fathers in Cultural Context.* New York: Routledge.
5. Martin, K. (1986). Adolescent pregnancy: the

perspective of the sisterhood of black single mothers, *J Community Health*. 11(1), 49–53.

6. Skinner, C. (2013). Child Maintenance Reforms: Understanding Fathers' Expressive Agency and the Power of Reciprocity. *International Journal of Law, Policy and the Family*. 27(2), 242–265.
7. Simpson, B., McCarthy, P., & Walker, J. (1995). *Being There: Fathers After Divorce*. Relate Centre for Family Studies: University of Newcastle.
8. Neale, B. (2016). Introduction: Young Fatherhood: Lived Experiences and Policy Challenges. *Social Policy and Society*. 15(1), 75–83.
9. Poole, E., Speight, S., O'Brien, M., Connolly, S., & Aldrich, M. (2016). Who are Non-Resident Fathers? A British Socio-Demographic Profile. *Journal of Social Policy*. 45 (2), 223–250.
10. The Centre for Social Justice (2020). *Facing the Facts: Ethnicity and Disadvantage in Britain Disparities in Education, Work, and Family*. London. www.centreforsocialjustice.org.uk
11. Ratele, K., & Nduna, M. (2018). An Overview of Fatherhood in South Africa. In W. Van den Berg & T, Makusha (Eds.), *State of South Africa's Fathers*. Cape Town: Sonke Gender Justice & Human Sciences Research Council.

12. Tach, L., Mincy, R., & Edin, K. (2010). Parenting as a "package deal": Relationships, fertility, and nonresident father involvement among unmarried parents. *Demography*. 47, 181–204.
13. Goldman, R., & Burgess, A. (2018). *Where's the daddy? Fathers and father-figures in UK datasets*. Fatherhood Institute. http://www.fatherhoodinstitute.org/wp-content/uploads/2017/12/Wheres-the-daddy-Executive-Summary-3.pdf
14. Carretié, L., Mercado, F., Tapia, M., & Hinojosa, J. A. (2001). Emotion, attention and the "negativity bias", studied through event-related potentials. *International Journal of Psychophysiology*. 41(1), 75–85.
15. Clowes, L., Ratele, K., & Shefer, T. (2013). Who needs a father? South African men reflect on being fathered *Journal of Gender Studies*. 22(3), 255–267.
16. McManus, A. (2021, January 26). *Wrinkly Fingers*. Annie MacManus. https://www.anniemacmanus.com/articles/wrinkly-fingers
17. Barras, J. R. (2000). *Whatever Happened to Daddy's Little Girl? The Impact of Fatherlessness on Black Women*. New York: Ballantine Publishing Group.

18. Johnson, E. (2020, January 31). *A dad explains: "Why I don't see my child"*. Wealthy Single Mommy. https://www.wealthysinglemommy.com/dads-explain-dont-see-kids/
19. Forsberg, H., & Autonen-Vaaraniemi, L. (2019). Moral orientations to post-divorce fatherhood: examining Finnish men's descriptive practices. *Families, Relationships and Societies*. 8(1), 23–36.
20. Cheadle, J. E., Amato, P. R., & King, V. (2010). Patterns of Nonresident Father Contact. *Demography*. 47(1), 205–225.
21. Parke, R. D. (1996). *Fatherhood.* Cambridge: Harvard University Press.
22. Tach, L., Mincy, R., & Edin, K. (2010). Parenting as a "package deal": Relationships, fertility, and nonresident father involvement among unmarried parents. *Demography*. 47, 181–204.
23. Geller, A. (2013). Paternal Incarceration and Father–Child Contact in Fragile Families. *Journal of Marriage & Family.* 75(5), 1288–1303.
24. Swisher, R. R., & Waller, M. R. (2008). Confining fatherhood: Incarceration and paternal involvement among nonresident White, African American, and Latino fathers. *Journal of Family Issues*. 29(8), 1067–1088.

25. Torabi, F. (2021). *This Mom Is Working to Help Divorced Women Achieve Financial Independence.* TIME. https://time.com/nextadvisor/in-the-news/closing-the-gap-shared-parenting/
26. Clawar, S. S., & Rivlin, B. (2014). *Children Held Hostage: Identifying Brainwashed Children, Presenting a Case, and Crafting Solutions.* US: American Bar Association.
27. Warshak, R. A. (2010). *Divorce Poison: How to Protect Your Family from Bad-mouthing and Brainwashing.* US: HarperCollins.
28. Harne, L. (2011). *Violent Fathering and the Risks to Children: The Need for Change.* Bristol: The Policy Press
29. Stark, E., & Hester, M. (2019). Coercive Control: Update and Review. *Violence Against Women.* 25(1), 81–104.
30. BBC News Report (2020, June 24). *Child maintenance: Mothers take legal action against DWP.* BBC News England. https://www.bbc.com/news/uk-england-53064741
31. Deighton Pierce Glynn Law (2020, June 21). *DPG instructed to challenge failures of the Child Maintenance Service.* Deighton Pierce Glynn News. https://dpglaw.co.uk/dpg-instructed-to-challenge-failures-of-the-child-maintenance-service/

FATHERS WITH SPUNK RISE: THE FUTURE

1. Buchanan, M. (2015, January 14). *'Feminists hate men': Meet Mike Buchanan, the leader of Britain's new Justice for Men and Boys party.* Independent.
2. https://www.independent.co.uk/news/people/feminists-hate-men-meet-mike-buchanan-the-leader-of-britain-s-new-justice-for-men-and-boys-party-9977357.html
3. Greig, A., & Edström, J. (2012). *Mobilising Men in Practice: Challenging sexual and gender-based violence in institutional settings.* Institute of Development Studies, Brighton: IDS.
4. Shapiro, J. (2021). *Father Figure: How to be a Feminist Dad.* New York: Little Brown & Company.
5. Wilson, J. (2021). *Battle Cry: Waging and Winning the War Within.* Nashville: Nelson Books.
6. Shapiro, J. (2021, February 3). *We Need More Feminist Dads.* Nautilus. https://nautil.us/issue/95/escape/i-want-to-be-a-feminist-dad
7. Cixous, C., Cohen, K., & Cohen, P. (1976). The Laugh of the Medusa, Signs. *The University of Chicago Press.* 1(4), 875–893.
8. Schneider, M, J. (@blcksmth). (2021, June

1). *"united we stand (feat. @linneasbg and @ kikisdmr. "Just because you experience a form of oppression doesn't mean you get to take part* [Photograph]. Instagram. https://www.instagram.com/p/CPi784UByFd/

9. Butcher, J. (2021, June 23). *Let's hear it for the men…* Jess Butcher Newsletter. https://jessbutcher.substack.com/p/lets-hear-it-for-the-men
10. Lamont, T. (2021, August 1). *How to raise a boy: my mission to bring up a son fit for the 21st century.* The Observer. https://www.theguardian.com/lifeandstyle/2021/aug/01/how-to-raise-a-boy-my-mission-to-bring-up-a-son-fit-for-the-21st-century

APPENDIX
The SPUNK SURVEY questionnaire

1. To start, could you tell us your age?
2. Which gender do you identify with the most?
3. Do you currently live with a partner?
4. Do you have any disabilities?
5. Which of the following most accurately describes the home you were raised in?
   a. Two-parent home: mother/father; Father/father; Mother/mother
   b. One parent home: single mother/single father
   c. Under care of the local authority
   d. Other – Write In
   e. Prefer not to say
6. Did you have any household responsibility as a child?
7. Do you have children? (Please include stepchildren)
8. How many children or stepchildren under 18

do you have? (It doesn't matter if you don't live with them)

9. How many sons do you have? (Please include stepsons)
10. How many daughters do you have? (Please include stepdaughters)
11. Do any of your children have disabilities?
12. How many different partners have you had children with?
13. How many stepchildren have you fathered?
14. How many children have you been a father figure for?
15. Are you a non-resident father for any of your children?
16. How many children under 18 do you live with more than 50% of the time?
17. How many children over 18 do you live with more than 50% of the time?
18. What do you enjoy the most about being a father?
19. What matters to you most as a father?
20. What do you consider to be good fathering?
21. What do you consider to be bad fathering?
22. In one phrase, how would you describe the mother(s) of your child/children?
23. What do you consider to be good mothering?
24. What do you consider to be bad mothering?

25. On your easiest day as a father, how adequate do you feel on a scale of 1 to 10?
26. On your hardest day as a father, how adequate do you feel on a scale of 1 to 10?
27. For the following statements, please indicate how much do you agree with each of them:
    a. I am a good father.
    b. I feel confident in my role as a father.
    c. Being a father is harder than being at work.
    d. I am the best father I can be.
    e. I am happy with the way that fatherhood is viewed by society.
    f. The mother(s) of my children think(s) I am a good father.
    g. Society expects more of mothers than of fathers in the role of parent.
    h. Work or studies make it harder to be a father.
    i. Being a father is harder than I thought it would be.
    j. I feel overwhelmed by my responsibilities as a father.
    k. A man can be a good father even if he doesn't live with his child.
    l. I know what it takes to be a good father.
    m. I have experienced depression due to fatherhood.

   n. My job allowed me to take paternity leave when my children were born.

28. What do you consider is the biggest barrier to being a good father?
29. What do you think is the difference between involved fathering and engaged fathering?
30. Using the scale provided, select the number that best describes how confident you feel in each situation, even if it is something that rarely occurs or does not concern you:
    a. Encouraged your child to ask questions about sexuality
    b. Started up a conversation about sexuality with your child
    c. Listened to your child's views on sexuality
    d. Felt comfortable in talking to your child about sexuality
    e. Encouraged your child to share their thoughts and feelings about sexuality
    f. Monitored your child's internet and television use
    g. You feel that you have adequate knowledge to provide sexuality education to your children
31. Do you ever feel mocked or ridiculed as a father?
32. In what ways do you feel, or have experienced

your fathering, or fathering in general, being mocked or ridiculed?

33. In three words, what fatherly role did you imagine you would take?
    a. First word:
    b. Second word:
    c. Third word:
34. Which three words describe your actual experience of being a father?
    ai. First word:
    aj. Second word:
    ak. Third word:
35. Fast forward twenty years and fatherhood has changed for the better. What changes have happened to make this so?
36. Since having your last child/children, do you have a new partner?
37. In your opinion, which statement most accurately describes your spouse/partner's involvement in your children's lives (whether a new or existing partner)
38. For the following statements, please indicate how much do you agree with each of them:
    a. I encourage my children to have a positive outlook on body image.
    b. I call out stereotypes when I see them.
    c. I avoid stereotypes in my children's media.

d. I feel comfortable with the shape of my body and my face.

39. How many (waking) hours per week do you see your children?
40. How many days per month do you see your children?
41. For the following statements, please indicate how much do you agree with each of them:
    a. I am doing my best to (re)connect with my children.
    b. The mother(s) of my children wants me to (re)connect with my children.
    c. It is too late to reunite with my children.
    d. The mother(s) of my children does not want me to (re)connect with my children.
42. Please rate these activities by how much participation you have in your role as a father for the children you live with or most recently lived with.
    aq. Dressing & undressing children/ Monitoring whether your children are appropriately dressed.
    ar. Pushing of clothes.
    as. Disposal of clothes when they have outgrown them.
    at. Washing, drying, ironing & putting away clothes for your children.